Reiki for Beginners

Unlock the Power of Palm Healing and Learn about Aura Cleansing, Chakra Healing, Meditation, and Developing Psychic Abilities

© Copyright 2021 — All rights reserved.

The contents of this book may not be reproduced, duplicated, or transmitted without direct written permission from the author.

Under no circumstances will any legal responsibility or blame be held against the publisher for any reparation, damages, or monetary loss due to the information herein, either directly or indirectly.

Legal Notice:

This book is copyright protected. This is only for personal use. You cannot amend, distribute, sell, use, quote or paraphrase any part or the content within this book without the consent of the author.

Disclaimer Notice:

Please note the information contained within this document is for educational and entertainment purposes only. Every attempt has been made to provide accurate, up to date and reliable complete information. No warranties of any kind are expressed or implied. Readers acknowledge that the author is not engaging in the rendering of legal, financial, medical, or professional advice. The content of this book has been derived from various sources. Please consult a licensed professional before attempting any techniques outlined in this book.

By reading this document, the reader agrees that under no circumstances is the author responsible for any losses, direct or indirect, which are incurred as a result of the use of information contained within this document, including, but not limited to, —errors, omissions, or inaccuracies.

Your Free Gift (only available for a limited time)

Thanks for getting this book! If you want to learn more about various spirituality topics, then join Mari Silva's community and get a free guided meditation MP3 for awakening your third eye. This guided meditation mp3 is designed to open and strengthen ones third eye so you can experience a higher state of consciousness. Simply visit the link below the image to get started.

https://spiritualityspot.com/meditation

Table of Contents

INTRODUCTION 1
CHAPTER 1: PALM HEALING EXPLAINED 3
    History of Palm Healing 4
    Hands and Our Natural Response to Pain 5
    Developing the Power of Healing 6
    Holistic Healing 6
    Prana/Chi 8
    The Pranic Body 10
CHAPTER 2: STARTING WITH MEDITATION 12
    What Is Meditation? 12
    Meditation and Reiki 14
    Benefits of Meditation 16
    Tips for Better Meditation 17
    The Biological and Neurological Effects of Meditation 18
CHAPTER 3: SENSING ENERGY, CHAKRAS, AND THE AURA 21
    The Energetic Anatomy 21
    Etheric Fields 22
    Morphogenetic Fields 22
    Special Energy Field 23
    The Aura 24
    What Is the Auric Field? 25

THE AURIC FIELD AND THE TWELVE CHAKRAS 27
THE SEVEN CHAKRAS 28
SENSING CHAKRAS 35
USING HANDS TO SENSE CHAKRAS 36
EXERCISES 38
CREATING AN ENERGY BALL 39
HAND CHAKRAS 40
OPENING THE CHAKRAS 42
OPENING THE ROOT CHAKRA 42
OPENING THE SACRAL CHAKRA 43
OPENING THE NAVEL CHAKRA 44
OPENING THE HEART CHAKRA 44
OPENING THE THROAT CHAKRA 45
OPENING THE THIRD EYE CHAKRA 45
OPENING THE CROWN CHAKRA 46

CHAPTER 4: PSYCHIC ABILITIES IN HEALING 47
DEVELOPING YOUR PSYCHIC ABILITIES 48
EXERCISES THAT HELP YOU DEVELOP CLAIRVOYANCE 51

CHAPTER 5: THE REIKI METHOD 57
A BRIEF HISTORY OF REIKI 57
THE ESSENCE OF REIKI 58
BENEFITS OF REIKI HEALING 60
REIKI METHODS 62
CLEARING THE SPACE WITH REIKI 62
USING THE REIKI BOX 63
USING THE REIKI BOX 64

CHAPTER 6: SCANNING THE AURA 66
A BRIEF HISTORY OF AURAS 66
WHAT IS AN AURA 67
AURA COLORS AND THEIR MEANINGS 68
HOW TO "READ" AURAS 69
HOW TO "INTERPRET" AURAS 70
REIKI AND SCANNING AURAS 71
HOW TO "FEEL" AURAS 73

CHAPTER 7: SELF-HEALING TECHNIQUES 75
- Connecting With the Energy of Reiki 75
- Scanning the Aura 78
- Activation of Reiki Symbols 79
- Setting an Intention 81
- Energy Guidance 82
- Close the Connection 82

CHAPTER 8: HEALING OTHERS 84
- Hands-on Healing 84
- Distant Healing 86

CHAPTER 9: RECEIVING YOUR FIRST REIKI ATTUNEMENT 90
- What Is a Reiki Attunement? 90
- Preparing for the First Attunement 92
- Tips for Increasing the Effectiveness of the Attunement 94
- How to Find a Qualified Reiki Healer? 94
- Evaluating Their Qualifications 95

CHAPTER 10: REIKI FOR DAILY WELL-BEING 99
- Habits to Improve Your Reiki Practice 99
- Here Are Some Easy Ways to Practice Reiki Daily 100

CONCLUSION 102

HERE'S ANOTHER BOOK BY MARI SILVA THAT YOU MIGHT LIKE 103

YOUR FREE GIFT (ONLY AVAILABLE FOR A LIMITED TIME) 104

BIBLIOGRAPHY 105

Introduction

Have you ever tried Reiki on yourself or tried giving it to someone? Maybe you heard about it from a friend? Whatever your reason for reading this, being interested in learning Reiki is already one step in the right direction. Once you learn the art of Reiki, it becomes a part of you and your life. It is a holistic healing method that has existed for a long time—it's a form of energy healing and is usually carried out using the palms of your hands. This is why it's often called palm healing. The term Reiki comes from two Japanese words, "Rei" and "Ki." Rei means soul or spirit, and Ki means vital energy.

The origins of Reiki are traced back to India and Japan, and most of the written information about it has still not been translated from its original languages. Much of it has been passed orally through practical experience, which is how it reached the West.

The practice of this healing form was started by Mikao Usui in the 1800s, who then taught it to over 2,000 students during his lifetime. However, Reiki's existence is a lot older than that. Over the years, more and more people have learned Reiki and made it a popular way to heal through universal energy or life force. As you read this book, you will learn all about what it is and what it can do.

This book aims to help you understand what Reiki is and how it can benefit you. You will learn much about your body and the energy system crucial for your well-being. However, mastering the art of this takes a lot of time and practice.

Do not give up even if you cannot see any substantial results at first. The ability to heal must be acquired with practice, patience, perseverance, and an open heart. Thus, start reading and watch as you become a Reiki healer much sooner than you ever expected.

Chapter 1: Palm Healing Explained

First, we will define and describe palm healing, also known as "the laying on of hands," which Reiki is more commonly known for across the world in various cultures. You will learn about the history of this type of healing without necessarily getting into Reiki just yet.

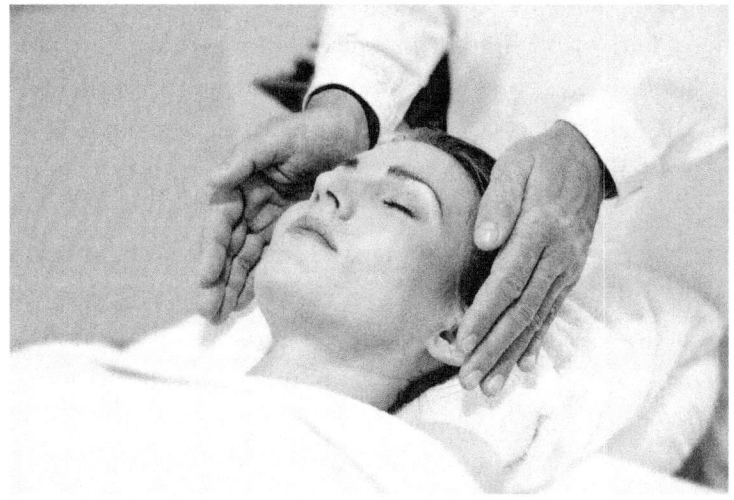

https://pixabay.com/sv/photos/v%C3%A4lbefinnande-massage-kvinna-285590/

History of Palm Healing

Palm healing has a long history. Different monarchies and religious groups have often claimed exclusive intellectual rights to its gifts, yet the basic truth is that every person has an innate ability to heal through energy flow. Through years of evolution, the human body has developed its ability to protect itself. For instance, when your skin gets cut, it automatically develops a protective layer known as the scab or clot. This scab protects the wound while the skin reconstructs itself under the scab, which is eventually peeled away to reveal brand-new skin underneath it.

Another defense/healing mechanism our body has developed is a fever. Firstly, the presence of a fever indicates an inflammation in the body. Secondly, it starts the production of an antidote by triggering the immune system into action to fight against the inflammation. When your body is pushed into extreme situations, it enters damage control mode and finds all manner of ways for it to carry on functioning during times of duress.

The best example of this ability is the "fight or flight" response hardwired into every human psyche. Under stressful situations, the hypothalamus reacts and releases chemicals into the body, which prepare it to either face the problem or run away from it. These are just some of the natural abilities that our bodies use to respond to distress.

Since the beginning of humankind and until the present day, humans have been making developments at an unprecedented speed. One exception to this is in the field of sensory observation and the paranormal. Today, only a few rare individuals have honed their ability to receive information without using any of the five primary sensory inputs. Over time, humans have generally lost their connection with nature but have gradually gained new skills and abilities.

Years ago, we could connect with nature and energies beyond the physical realm. Before the advent of colonization and scientific learning, humans had a strong contact with nature, and we were highly in tune with the spiritual energies of the world. This was essential when it came to survival—since early humans wandered through places in search of food and shelter and had to be skilled at avoiding predators and other life-threatening dangers.

With the advancement of civilization, humans have increasingly ignored these signals and instructions from nature sourced from a higher plane beyond this earthy realm that helped them survive in hostile environments. Humans became increasingly insensitive to the subtle signals given off by the earth and nature, which we still receive sometimes through auras but battle to perceive.

Historically speaking, Master Usui, who taught Reiki, was also famous for teaching tenohira (palm healing) and different forms of meditation. While collaborating with the naval officers of the Japanese army, Usui began teaching the use of tenohira as an addition to first aid. Then, Hayashi Chujiro, a naval surgeon, expanded on the different positions of hand placement used for modern-day palm healing.

Hands and Our Natural Response to Pain

When we sense pain, we immediately place our hands on that part of our body, hoping to alleviate the pain. This reaction is based on pure instinct. If you have a terrible backache, you will immediately put your hands there without even thinking about why you are doing it. Another similar reflex is blinking; we instinctively close our eyes when something flies toward our face.

Most would say they are simply trying to make themselves feel better by massaging these sore spots with their hands. Another explanation is that human beings have been able to heal with bioenergy since the dawn of humankind, but only a few individuals can still do it today. Everyone can use their hands for healing purposes, regardless of their age or experience. Factors like intelligence, social status, ethnicity, and religious affiliation have nothing to do with anyone's ability to heal with their hands.

Developing the Power of Healing

When we are born, our healing power is exceptionally low, and if we do not develop it, it will remain at the same level. If you consistently exercise your healing power, it will increase in power and remain so for the rest of your life. People gifted with more bioenergy power have a greater advantage, as it will take them a shorter time to heal another person. To begin healing, you don't need to have your healing powers developed to a maximum level.

When you place your palms over a sore spot to heal it, healing begins instantly. Even though your initial efforts may feel weak, the results are immediate, even though they may be very modest at first. With each subsequent pass of your hand, the flow of your bioenergy becomes stronger, and your ability to heal gets stronger.

Just as one might not need an understanding of the laws of gravity to understand that it exists, one does not need to grasp the concept of energy healing to practice palm healing. Visiting a palm healer or an energy healer can do wonders for you—if you go with an open mind. If you are suffering from stress, anxiety, or other issues, a palm-healing session can help you balance your energy levels so that you can feel good, and if you are already feeling good, it is still possible to feel a little bit better. Just as we brush our hair or take a bath every day, cleansing your energy regularly is also necessary. Sometimes people also practice smudging or burning sage to help remove the negativity from their energy field at the same time as palm healing.

Holistic Healing

Holistic healing involves all the necessary tools to help an individual find a source of personal power. When we achieve personal power, we can dictate our thoughts, which lets us imagine a better life and helps manifest it. Holistic healing is all about finding inner peace, happiness, and experiencing complete wellness. Although that may seem quite philosophical and thought-provoking to a layman, it is the essence of holistic healing.

In simpler terms, holistic healing is the practice of healing a person while looking at the person as a whole and not just solely focusing on their physical symptoms. If you look at the definition according to the dictionary, holistic healing is "characterized by the holistic treatment of the person as a whole person while taking into account all the social and mental factors affecting them instead of focusing purely on the symptoms of the disease."

Many people often fail to find proper relief for their ailments, which forces them to start exploring other avenues of treatment, leading them toward a holistic lifestyle and alternative treatments offering relief and healing. Often, many people mix up holistic healing with "alternative medicine," "integrative medicine," or "complementary medicine." Although all of them may not be the same thing, what distinguishes each as separate is the focus of the treatment.

Current medical treatment focuses on physical symptoms. In holistic healing, the healer focuses on all the aspects of a person—hence the term holistic, the goal of which is to establish a balance and harmony in the mind, body, and spirit. Whether we are aware of it or not, life and the different situations that it brings forth causes us to respond to situations in different ways, be it physically, mentally, spiritually, or emotionally.

Western medicine and other conventional medical practices view the body as a separate entity from the rest of our being. The approach of holistic healing views the body as a reflection of the person as a whole. Holistic healing does not focus on "me and my body"; instead, it stresses "I am my body." Thus, the mind and body are a single entity.

A healer needs to listen to what the patient is saying, but more importantly, what is not being said— "listening between the lines"—and this information must be integrated into the patient's life situation. Healers need to recognize the discomfort or symptoms of an underlying problem, whether physical or emotional. For example, if a person has insomnia because of anxiety or stress, prescribing sleeping pills is of no use. This will simply mask the real symptoms of a deep-rooted problem and will fail to heal their patient.

The person could become pill dependent, which, as we know, is not uncommon. Very soon, the lack of sleep leeches into other parts of the patient's life, causing further problems, burdening their mind even more. The cycle worsens, and eventually, the person's condition may deteriorate into something even worse than it was initially. In this case, the sleeping pills act as a short-term solution to a long-term problem, which should have otherwise been resolved through lifestyle changes and therapy.

Prana/Chi

Although Prana is more popular as a principle of yoga, it is something every individual has. Prana is the primordial energy of the universe, which flows through our bodies and is dispersed through the material realms. Steeped in Hinduism, Prana—or its Chinese counterpart, chi—is the life force or universal energy. It is the amalgamation of all the energy in the universe, including the dormant energies of nature. It's not something that can be easily perceived since it always remains in a static state, subtle and motionless. Prana or chi only enters a dynamic state when activated by vibrations and manifests itself as magnetism, light, heat, and electricity.

Prana comes from the Sanskrit word "pra," meaning ever constant, and "an," meaning dynamic. The etymology of the world is "constant movement," which is associated with the vibrational characteristics of all the different forms of energy. In Chinese, chi translates to energy. Thus, the entire universe is made of energy and matter. Charles

Darwin's Theory of Evolution suggests that all life forms originated from a single common source and that the diversification and different species adapted and evolved in response to environmental changes.

Similarly, energy is the source of all life forms, manifested into matter, creating all the rich contrasts and variations our world has to offer. We live in the physical realm where creation is propelled by dualities such as the concepts of yin and yang, the moon and the sun, and Shakti and Shiva. The concept of Prana is validated in modern science through Albert Einstein's Theory of Special Relativity. Einstein's theory suggests that matter and energy are the same physical entity and interchangeable. This means that the universe is created by energy, and we humans share this energy.

It infuses and vitalizes all forms of matter. It also merges into atoms and subatomic particles, which we already know are the building blocks of matter and manifestations of the physical realm. This means that every atom, subatomic particle, and cell is an extension of Prana/chi. Experts also believe that Prana/chi has an inherent intelligence, enabling it to perform life-sustaining processes.

What we breathe in is also considered to be another form of Prana. The physical breath corresponds to the movement of Prana into the astral spine. Prana flows up and down this astral spine, corresponding to inhalation and exhalation. The link between the flow of Prana and breathing patterns is the central pillar of many yoga and meditation techniques.

In Eastern medicine, chi is the vital energy flowing through the entire body. All the organ systems are connected through chi and are affected if a single part is suffering, so the whole body needs to be checked to find the root of the "dis - ease." The concept of Chinese medicine is that if your body is suffering from a disorder, your chi or life force is imbalanced, and the flow must be restored. Chi and Prana are essentially the same thing, so do not get confused when one is interchanged with the other. Acupuncture and Reiki healing are closely connected with chi and restore the proper flow of chi to alleviate symptoms and ailments.

Prana is not only a mere philosophical concept but also a physical substance in every sense. Just as electromagnetic waves and gravitational fields exist, so do the Pranic waves, fields, and chi exist in the body even though we cannot see them. Every single one of us has a specific quantity of Prana/chi in our bodies, and this life force is used for different activities during our day and our lifetime.

When Prana is diminished, ailments and disorders creep into the body. When we have ample chi/Prana in our body, our body stays in perfect health. When a person possesses an excess of chi/Prana, it can be transferred to other people and is used for healing (palm healing, Reiki healing).

Without Prana, a living being has no consciousness. Prana/chi is the basic building block of our holistic existence. For instance, a fetus will share its mother's Prana, and both exist as a singular entity of the universal consciousness before the third trimester. After the third trimester, the developing fetus develops its own consciousness and Prana.

All the activities we perform require Prana/chi—moving, speaking, using our senses, thinking, and existing. A healthy individual will have plenty of life force within them, and their bodies will have a proper flow of Prana. Most diseases, either physical or mental, are caused by the improper distribution of Prana or chi due to the blockage of chakra centers and energy channels.

The Pranic Body

In the human body, blood is constantly flowing through our veins, capillaries, and arteries. Similarly, in our Pranic body, Prana flows through energy channels and pathways called Nadis. Prana enters our body when we breathe in. When we practice breathing exercises and expand the breadth and quality of breathing, we simultaneously expand and improve our Prana and the quality of this vital life force.

This is why breathing techniques are such a big part of yoga and Pranayama.

Chakras or energy centers are also an important aspect of the Pranic body. There are seven chakra or energy centers that exist along the spine. In yoga, these are the prime focus. Each of these chakras is connected to different organs and specific glands of the body as well as different areas of our psyche, which influence our personality. Many people believe that health and well-being are improved when there is a balanced flow of energy through these seven important chakras. On the contrary, if Prana cannot flow through the body naturally—due to blockages or overstimulation—it can create an imbalance and disharmony, both on a biological and emotional level.

The channels that Prana flows through are a complex network of Nadis, where energy is sourced from the root chakra, also known as Muladhara, at the base of the spine. Nadi comes from the Sanskrit word Na, meaning flow. Among the different energy pathways, three primary Nadis are the main pathways for distributing chi or Prana to different parts and organ systems of the body. Minor Nadis branch out of these major Nadis and into every single part of the body. Yoga and holistic healing practices are directed toward creating a balance and ensuring the smooth flow of life force through the chakras.

Chapter 2: Starting with Meditation

In this chapter, we will study meditation. Knowing how to meditate effectively is essential to any kind of energy healing, as it puts the healer in a state of calm and enables him or her to pick up on unbalanced energies, tune in to the receiver of healing, and allow their own energy to flow optimally. As a Reiki practitioner, you will need to meditate prior to healing. Here you'll learn some meditation exercises you can use during a Reiki session.

What Is Meditation?

Meditation is one of the oldest techniques of memory improvement. It involves learning how to control your focus and attention, and if you cannot, you will never succeed when it comes to improving your memory. While meditating, you will have to calm yourself and keep your mind from wandering. Classic meditation requires you to empty your mind of all thoughts and distractions. You will need a quiet spot with no external distractions to meditate effectively. Meditation is a very simple practice, and all you need to do is keep the correct posture and concentrate on your breathing.

Meditation trains your mind to focus on the present moment. Relax your body, and listen to your breath while you concentrate on each inhale and exhale action. And while you are doing this, dissociate yourself from all your worries and regrets. However, it is easy to get distracted, but you must focus on the present moment. Initially, it's difficult, and you will find yourself distracted by thoughts. You'll notice that your mind will constantly attempt to interrupt you at every opportunity. Over time, you'll be able to empty your mind and focus on the present moment more easily. This is why meditation does not work unless you do it every day.

There are several methods. Each caters to different individuals on a personal level. Some people respond well to classical meditation, while others may find transcendental meditation more effective. If one form of meditation does not work for you, you can try switching to another form. When people hear the word "meditation," it instantly brings up the notion of sitting still while sitting in an incredibly uncomfortable half-lotus position and chanting the word "ohm" repeatedly.

This might work for some but may be useless for others. You need to find what works best for you and stick to that approach. It is possible to meditate while walking, floating on water, or lying down on a hammock. It's not always necessary for you to assume uncomfortable positions and chant mantras.

Experts suggest beginners start by meditating for five minutes. This may sound like a long time to sit and think of nothing, and it is true that when you first start, those five minutes will feel like ages. But five minutes is the perfect amount of time for a beginner. You might feel like giving up but persevere! Meditating for even one or two minutes can help you establish the habit and strengthen your cognitive powers.

Meditation and Reiki

Reiki meditation is a form of meditation where you feel the subtle life force energy—the Prana/chi—and practicing it can give you immense relief. Reiki meditation involves placing your hands on specific points on the body and visualizing symbols that facilitate healing experiences. Reiki healing is one of the oldest healing methods in the world of medicine. In a world full of negative energy and stress, our energy centers or chakras get blocked by the influence of stress and negative energies caused by day-to-day living. Reiki sessions help with many issues, such as stress and pain, and some claim they can even treat some of the most serious illnesses.

A lot of hospitals and healing centers offer Reiki as a supplementary therapy. If you are new to Reiki, the best way to begin is by finding a professional practitioner and getting some form of coaching or therapy sessions. Reiki meditation will help you unclog any energy blockages that might be present in your body and get the energy flowing through it the way it is supposed to. When energy begins to flow through your body, it can help establish harmony and eliminate all the imbalances that these energy blocks might have created. Chakras are not independent of each other, and they act as a whole unit. Each chakra can function properly only if the other chakras are aligned and clear of blockages.

To energize your chakras or even heal them through Reiki meditation, sit in a comfortable position, keeping your spine upright. Take in five to ten deep breaths and allow your body and mind to relax. You can even use chants such as "Om" or any mantra that appeals to you to enhance the relaxing effect. This will relax your mind, so your energies are in balance.

Once you have reached a peaceful state of mind, start meditating by focusing on the root chakra and gradually move your focus up toward the crown chakra. Placing your hands over the different chakra points can help you to enhance the healing effect of Reiki. Visualize the Reiki energy coursing through your hands and entering your body through the root chakra.

Another way of making the meditation more effective is to visualize the colors of the respective chakra points. For instance, if you are focusing on the root chakra, visualize the color red. Keep channeling the Reiki energy through your root chakra for three or four minutes. Once you are done, visualize your root chakra being strengthened and revitalized by the Reiki energy and all blockages being unblocked. Repeat the same process for all the seven chakras of your body and perform the same manifestation to cleanse your aura.

The use of healing crystals can also intensify your Reiki meditation sessions. For every chakra point, certain crystals amplify the vibrational frequency of your energy. If you are looking to use a single crystal, go for clear quartz, also known as the master crystal. The master crystal can help you heal all the seven chakra points simultaneously. The use of mantras and soft music can also complement your Reiki sessions.

Reiki meditation is considered a divine process, and it provides an effective way to find answers or seek guidance for issues that might be bothering you and thereby create an imbalance in your body. When you put your mind in a meditative state, the divine energy of the universe will try to communicate with you through different signs and symbols. These messages and signs can help you find the answers you are looking for, create positive changes within yourself, and facilitate healing and dealing with problems or issues that you might be facing.

Remember, meditation does not necessarily mean closing your eyes and reciting mantras or chants. Although this can help soften the mind and ground yourself, you can adopt any method that suits your personality. You can simply sit down and stare at a candle flame, or you can listen to calming sounds and let your mind zone out.

As with anything else, you can perform meditation daily or weekly. Trust yourself while doing it and listen to your intuition to identify things you need to focus on. For some people, it may be easy, and for others, it might take a while to overcome the initial struggle of letting go of thoughts. This is where consistency is important—the more you practice, the better you will get at it. It is also essential to keep track of your progress and note your progress weekly or monthly.

Meditating regularly will help you bring positive energy into your body and improve the flow of this energy through all the different chakras, creating a balance and ensuring that you have a healthy mind and body at the same time.

Benefits of Meditation

Improved Brain Activity

Improved cognition and neurological activity are some of the most effective ways of preventing the onset of neurodegenerative diseases such as Alzheimer's disease and Parkinson's disease. Meditation profoundly impacts memory, cognition, attention, and other brain functions that usually deteriorate and degenerate with the onset of old age. If you meditate regularly, your later years could be spent in a much better state of health, without the forgetfulness and mental deterioration that comes with old age.

Makes You Alert

Have you ever ordered a coffee without realizing you ordered the wrong kind? And you end up paying for a cappuccino while you prefer an espresso? Have you repeatedly lost track of time and were late to a dentist appointment? Or have you ever missed your exit on the highway because you were distracted? These minor setbacks add up to making your day problematic. These things are enough to ruin your day and, by extension, your mood. Meditation ensures that you are always aware of what is happening around you.

Better for Mental Health

Anxiety and depression are mental health disorders, but they are not caused by bacteria or viruses, unlike other health problems. They are caused by social anxiety and emotional stress. They have a terrible effect on your mind and quality of life, drastically reducing your life expectancy and longevity if not dealt with in time. This is why the treatment of anxiety and depression is not centered upon treating one part of the body.

Instead, the most effective way of making progress is by improving the overall quality of life by alleviating stressors that cause depression or anxiety. Meditation has a wholesome effect on the mind and, instead of targeting one condition, keeps your brain healthy and prevents neurodegeneration in older people.

Tips for Better Meditation

- When you meditate, judge nothing. Judging is what brings you back to the real world. Meditation requires that you be free to attribute any value to emotions, impulses, and feelings.
- Keeping your attention free is the aim of the whole process. It can also be achieved in small ways. As you meditate, consider what is happening outside of your body. The environment in which you meditate gives you various sensations in the form of sounds, images, and smells. Learn to witness all of this without distracting yourself from meditation.
- The approach is an essential part of mindfulness meditation. If simple things such as a low sound or a fly easily distract you, you will not be successful. Only by learning to ignore distractions can mindfulness meditation succeed.
- Do not give up if you initially fail. It is not the same for everyone. Some people find it a breeze, while others are easily distracted. The key is to keep trying. The more you try, the better you will be.
- Transform your emotions. Negative emotions such as anger, irritation, and jealousy can be redirected so that you think about more positive things. Stand away from them, looking in silence. Watch them try to play tricks on your mind and do not say a word.

- The ancient saints and ascetics of the East used meditation to stay in shape, endured the most brutal climate, and lived frugal lives. They read many scriptures and recited them verbatim after the first reading. How do you think it was possible? The answer is meditation.
- A cross-legged position is the best for meditation. The ancient sages who achieved supreme happiness, also known as Nirvana, felt that a cross-legged position offered many opportunities. It is also considered the best position to take your meal. This position also helps you stay upright, focused, and attentive—all the desirable conditions for an ideal meditation.

The Biological and Neurological Effects of Meditation

Better Limbic Functions

Meditation also profoundly affects limbic function, verbal fluency, and increases flexibility in cognitive functions. People are increasingly suffering from mental health disorders, neurodegenerative diseases, and personality dissociation disorders caused by a decline in healthy lifestyle choices and poor dietary practices.

The use of devices such as mobile phones and computers can also reduce the attention span of young children and prevent the proper development of the brain. Since most of the population is desensitized toward using mobile phones and gadgets and is constantly being dissociated from their surroundings, this restricts the development of neurons in certain regions of the brain. These underdeveloped regions of the brain can lack cognitive function, increasing the risk of developing neurological disorders. With the increased numbers of mental health disorders and neurological diseases, meditation has become a powerful tool that is freely available for everyone to use.

Although many scientists are studying the process of meditation and its effects on the body, there are no conclusive and definitive proofs to quantify this. In a spiritual context, meditation has proved to be a powerful tool in expanding consciousness and developing spirituality. The inner peace and positive emotions experienced after a good meditation session improve brain waves in your cerebral cortex and cognitive pathways.

There have also been some research studies that investigated the effects of meditation on abnormal aging and neurodegeneration. Practices such as transcendental meditation and mindfulness stimulate the production of neurological connections and neurochemical receptors in your brain.

Some MRI studies have also shown that the brain undergoes an actual morphological change that is visible in these scans. It was found that seniors who practiced meditation daily had a significantly increased thickness of the cerebral cortex. These neurons also made structural changes and showed an alteration in different regions of the brain, such as the superior and inferior prefrontal cortex, the frontal cortex, the anterior cingulate cortex, and the amygdala. These regions of the brain are associated with performing different cognitive functions, such as sensory processing, attention, limbic response, and other executive functions.

Studies also show that daily meditation results in a significant increase in the volume of suprachiasmatic nuclei in the hippocampus region of the brain. The hippocampus is responsible for memory and sensory function, and an increase in the suprachiasmatic nuclei increases the functional capacity of the hippocampus.

The most profound effect of meditation was observed in older adults. The increase in the thickness of the prefrontal cortex was much more significant in people over the age of 60, as opposed to their younger counterparts. This was a strong indicator that the practice of meditation can have a compensatory effect on neurodegeneration and showed a decrease in thickness of the cerebral cortex that is brought about by old age. The increase in the thickness of the cerebral cortex can be attributed to several different factors, such as the multiplication of glial cells, neuronal arborization, and an increase in the number of blood vessels in the brain. This is a strong argument for meditation as a method of neuroregeneration.

There is insufficient information and research on the actual effects of meditation to make a definitive generalization regarding the results that it may provide. All research studies conducted to study the effects of meditation on the brain suggest that these benefits are real and not just a placebo effect. The mechanism of these effects and why it works has been attributed to one factor: the cerebral perfusion of the parietal lobe, prefrontal cortex, and auditory cortex. This has a protective effect on the thickness of the gray matter of the cerebral cortex.

Better Cognition

The positive health benefits of meditational practices on various aspects, such as physical and mental health, are receiving more attention, particularly with the advent of the Internet and ease of access to information. The evidence is provided in many medical research studies, which show a high correlation between meditation and improved cognitive functional capacity and the efficiency of cognition itself. Improved cognition and neurological activity in the brain are the most effective ways to prevent the onset of neurodegenerative diseases such as Alzheimer's and Parkinson's. Meditation profoundly impacts memory, cognition, attention, and other functions that usually deteriorate and degenerate with the onset of old age.

Chapter 3: Sensing Energy, Chakras, and the Aura

Now let us get into the topic of energy. Here you will learn more about energy, the energy field, the chakra system, as well as energy bodies, with each explained in detail. Then we will get into the subject of the aura—what it is, how it functions, and what it means. Toward the end of this section, we have provided exercises on sensing energy, creating an energy ball, opening the chakras, and seeing auras. All this knowledge is necessary to become a healer and identify problematic areas in the body/aura.

The Energetic Anatomy

There are many types of human energy fields. They include the measurable magnetic and electromagnetic fields generated by every living cell, organ, tissue, and body. They also include biofields that are subtle fields radiating from the pulsing units of living things along with our energy bodies and channels.

Etheric Fields

Etheric is a word that usually replaces aura or subtle body. Independent etheric fields are present around all vibrating units of life. This applies to cells, people, and even plants. A specific etheric field is also connected to your body. This term was derived from the word "ether"—something that can permeate through space while transmitting waves of energy transversely. An etheric field surrounds the entire body, and therefore it is an important part of a person's energy field. The popular view is to consider it a separate energy body, and it's said to link other bodies to the physical body. Barbara Brennan, an expert on the aura, suggests that the human energy field exists before the growth of cells. Phoebe Bendit, a renowned author and clairvoyant, says the same of the auric field, and she believes that it acts as a matrix while permeating every particle in the body. The etheric body is linked to the meridians; however, Dr. Kim Bonghan, an expert in acupuncture, suggests that these meridians act as an interface between the physical body and the etheric energy field.

Morphogenetic Fields

A morphogenetic field refers to a group of cells forming an organ or a body structure. For example, heart tissue is formed from a cardiac field. In the 1980s, Rupert Sheldrake, an English biologist, first labeled learning fields that instructed the ones recognized scientifically. He called them morphic, energetic, or subtle morphogenetic fields. He also suggested that an energy field is present around and within a morphic unit. Every living organism belonging to a specific group will tune in to that morphic field and develop through morphic resonance. This resonance will only take place between similar forms. This means that a plant cannot take up the characteristics of a rabbit.

Sheldrake also said these energy fields acted like a mental database. His theory explains why certain emotions, behaviors, and other characteristics are passed down in a family. Many studies have shown that members of the same species will acquire similar behavior or traits even when separated, and morphogenetic fields could explain this. His philosophy also stated that the morphic energy field of a soul could carry past life memories from one lifetime to another. These memories would not be local, and they would not be anchored in a particular life or your brain.

Special Energy Field

Various biofields regulate different emotional, spiritual, mental, and physical functions. The fields correspond accordingly to the different parts of the subtle body:

- The physical field has the lowest frequency and regulates the physical body of a person.
- An etheric field is like a blueprint of the physical body that it surrounds. The soul has an etheric human energy field as well.
- The emotional field regulates the emotions of the organism.
- The mental field processes a person's beliefs, thoughts, and ideas.
- The astral field is free of space and time. This nexus is between the spiritual and physical realm.
- An etheric template lies only in a spiritual place and has high existential ideals.
- Celestial fields act as a template for etheric fields and can access universal energies.
- Causal fields will direct the lower existence levels.

The Aura

For hundreds of years, scientists have been researching the existence of the aura that surrounds every living body. This human energy field has auric fields or auric layers made of bands of energy. They connect us to the world and surround the subtle body. Different cultures call the aura by different names. It is known as an astral light by the Kabbalists. In Christianity, you see it as the rings of light or halos around Jesus and other holy figures. The human energy field is described in much more detail in Vedic scriptures and teachings by Buddhists, Native Americans, and Rosicrucians. Pythagoras saw it as a luminous body and discussed this field, too.

Since the early 1800s, there has been active scientific interest in the mystery of the aura. At the time, Jan Baptist van Helmont, a prominent chemist and physiologist, saw it as some universal fluid that could permeate everything. Throughout history, it has been said that the aura is considered as something that flows and is permeable. Franz Mesmer, the founder of the study of hypnosis, suggested that a magnetic fluid charges inanimate and animate objects and that material bodies can influence each other through this fluid.

Several unique properties of this energy field were also discovered by Baron Wilhelm von Reichenbach. In his research as a geologist, meteorologist, and philosopher, he called the aura the Odic force, which would later be known as the subtle body. He found that the Odic force had properties like an electromagnetic field. It has opposites or polarities, just like the electromagnetic field did.

In the odic field, he understood that like attracts like, while in electromagnetism, opposites will attract each other. Von Reichenbach also found that this field could flow around objects, carry a charge, and relate to various colors. According to his beliefs, the odic field on the left half of the body was a negative pole, while the right half was a positive pole. Many other theories stated that the aura was flowing or fluid and consisted of many colors while being magnetic and permeable.

For instance, in other research, Dr. Walter Kilner, a medical electrician, used colored filters and a specific type of coal tar to examine the aura in 1911. Through this, he discovered three zones. One was a dark layer right next to a person's skin. Another was an ethereal layer that was flowing perpendicularly to the body. The third was a delicate exterior that had about six inches of contours.

More importantly, he found that the aura shifts its condition in reaction to the subject's state of mind and health. Our knowledge about this human energy field was further expanded by Dr. Wilhelm Reich in the early 1900s. He used experiments to study the qualities of the universal energy he called "orgone."

According to several metaphysicians, this organ was the same as Prana or chi. Reich observed energy pulsing around animate and inanimate subjects during his studies. He also found that change could be brought about by clearing areas of congestion and releasing any negative emotional or mental patterns. This demonstrated the connection between physical energies and the subtle body, as well as the connection with mental and emotional energies.

What Is the Auric Field?

We now know that the auric field exists, but what exactly is it? Scientists say that it is a bio-magnetic field surrounding the body. The laws of physics clearly state that energy fields are not bounded. This means that there is no limit to how far our bio-magnetic human energy field can extend. Modern equipment allows us to measure the heart's energy fields up to fifteen feet in distance. This field is the strongest compared to others from different organs. According to science, the function of the aura is to convey information about what takes place within the body rather than what happens on the skin. This is why the aura is vital for internal health monitoring and function.

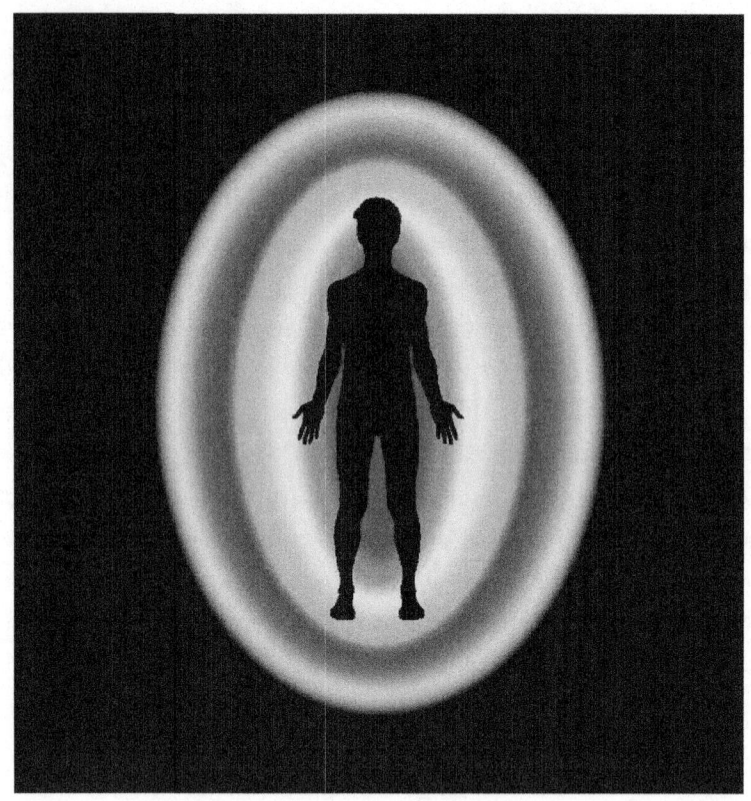

https://pixabay.com/sv/illustrations/aura-chakra-att-f%C3%A4rga-esoterisk-1079745/

This biomagnetic field contains information about every organ and tissue in the body. The currents of the heart determine its shape since this organ is the strongest. The circulatory system establishes the primary electrical flow. The circulatory system interacts with the nervous system, and distinct flows are created. These appear like whirling patterns in the field. It is not possible to completely understand the aura's purpose without learning about what it comprises. There is still much more knowledge to be gained regarding what the aura is made of.

Barbara Ann Brennan, the founder of Brennan Healing Science and a physicist, states that the aura is made of bioplasma, which is the fifth state of matter. These bioplasma particles could be subatomic and move in clouds. According to the philosopher Rudolf Steiner, ether is what makes up the aura. It is an element like hollow space or a negative mass. It can be surmised that the human energy field might be made of antimatter, allowing an energy shift between worlds as well as electromagnetic radiation. Thus, to deliver healing, healers have to create a lot of intensity in the energies of the here and now to access the same in the anti-worlds. What is accomplished in one's own field can be sent across to the energy field of another like a message.

Brennan proposed that there are seven layers to this auric field. These layers are linked with the chakras and graduate from your body. The seven chakras are also attuned to the subtle bodies and combine to form three planes. These are accessible from the auric fields. She intuitively perceived two levels that are beyond the etheric and called them the cosmic plane. These are associated with the eighth and ninth chakras. She says that the ninth has a crystalline template while the eighth is fluid.

The Auric Field and the Twelve Chakras

The twelve chakra system theory makes Brennan's claims about the eighth and ninth chakras seem valid. The auric fields are connected to these chakras and connect what happens within and outside of the body.

The Seven Chakras

You may or may not be familiar with the concept of chakras but, as a Reiki healer, you need to understand the basics about them.

https://commons.wikimedia.org/wiki/File:Chakras_map.svg

A chakra is a Sanskrit term that means wheel. The chakras in the body are imagined like free-flowing wheels of energy. There are seven chakras in the body, and these chakras are energy centers. The chakras correspond to different parts of your body and have different functions.

Energy flows through each chakra, and when they are all open, there is a steady flow of energy, ensuring your well-being. It allows harmony between the mind, body, and spirit. However, if one or more of your chakras is blocked, underactive, or overactive, balance is disturbed, which will negatively manifest in your mind, body, or spirit.

Now let us learn about each chakra individually:

Muladhara or the Root Chakra

The root chakra signifies the foundation of a person. It is located at the base of your spine. When it is open, you will feel grounded. You will feel confident and as if you can overcome any challenges in life. When the chakra is blocked, you will feel insecure and unsure of yourself and your abilities. The color representing this chakra is red, and the stone is hematite. The earth element is linked to the root chakra and practicing the Warrior 1 yoga pose will help you open this chakra.

Image: Muladhara or Root Chakra

Svadhisthana or the Sacral Chakra

The sacral chakra is present a couple of inches below your navel, in the lower abdomen. It controls your creativity, sexual energy, and emotions. When this chakra is blocked, you will feel like you have no control over your life. The color representing this chakra is orange, and the stone is a tiger's eye. The water element is linked to it, and practicing the Bound Angle yoga pose will help you open the chakra.

Mirzolot2, CC BY-SA 3.0 https://creativecommons.org/licenses/by-sa/3.0
via Wikimedia Commons
https://commons.wikimedia.org/wiki/File:Swadhisthana.svg
Image: Svadhisthana or Sacral Chakra

Manipura or the Solar Plexus Chakra

The solar plexus chakra is the third chakra in your body, and it is in the upper abdomen around your stomach. This chakra controls your sense of self-esteem, self-confidence, and self-worth. Have you ever felt like there were butterflies in your stomach or maybe a pit sitting heavily in it? This is because of the solar plexus chakra. When it is blocked, you will doubt yourself and feel overwhelming shame. If the chakra is open, you will be confident enough to express your true self. The color representing this chakra is yellow, and the stone is amber. The element is fire, and practicing the Boat Pose will be helpful to create a free flow of energy through the chakra.

Mirzolot2, CC BY-SA 3.0 htttps://creativecommons.org/licenses/by-sa/3.0 via Wikimedia Commons
https://commons.wikimedia.org/wiki/File:Manipura.svg

Image: Manipura or Solar Plexus Chakra

Anahata or the Heart Chakra

The heart chakra acts as a bridge between the upper and lower chakras in your body. The upper chakras are linked to spirituality, while the lower chakras are linked to materiality. This chakra influences how you receive or give love. When it is blocked, you will find it difficult to open up to people. When the heart chakra is open, you will be empathetic and have deep compassion for others. You will also be much more open to receiving love from others. The color representing this chakra is green, and the stone is rose quartz. The air element is linked to it, and practicing the Camel Pose in yoga will help you develop this chakra.

https://en.m.wikipedia.org/wiki/File:Chakra4.svg

Image: Anahata or Heart Chakra

Vishuddha or the Throat Chakra

The throat chakra acts as the voice for your heart chakra. It controls your ability to speak the truth, express yourself, and communicate with others. When the chakra is open, you will find it easy to voice your thoughts and opinions clearly and truly. When the throat chakra is blocked, you will find it difficult to express what you want to say. The color representing this chakra is light blue or turquoise. The element is sound or music. Aquamarine is the stone linked to this chakra, and practicing the Fish Pose in yoga will be beneficial.

https://en.m.wikipedia.org/wiki/File:Chakra5.svg
Image: Vishuddha or Throat Chakra

Ajna or the Third Eye Chakra

The further up you move in the chakra system, the more you connect with the divine. This chakra is present between your eyes and is connected to your intuition. It will control your wisdom and imagination. This chakra can take in information that lies beyond the surface. If your third eye chakra is completely open, you may experience visions or have a very apt intuitive ability. The color representing this chakra is dark blue or purple, and the stone is amethyst. The element linked to it is light, and practicing the child's pose in yoga will help to strengthen this chakra.

https://en.m.wikipedia.org/wiki/File:Chakra6.svg
Image: Ajna or Third Eye Chakra

Sahasrara or the Crown Chakra

The crown chakra lies at the crown of your head. It controls the ability of a person to connect spiritually to the universe. It is linked to both inner and outer beauty. If this chakra is open, it allows you to access a very high consciousness level. It is rare to find people who have an open crown chakra. The color representing this chakra is violet or white, and the stone is clear quartz. The element of divine consciousness is linked to this chakra, and practicing the headstand yoga pose will strengthen this chakra.

https://en.m.wikipedia.org/wiki/File:Chakra7.svg
Image: Sahasrara or Crown Chakra

Sensing Chakras

Learning to sense chakras is a part of energy healing as well. These energy centers are like portals in the energy field of a person. These vortices allow energy to flow in and out of your body. The seven major chakras in your body are linked to specific organs, glands, and other aspects of your body. Other than the major ones, there are other minor chakras. When there is a disturbance in the flow of energy through your chakras, it impacts your mind, body, spirit, and life in many ways. This is why energy healers work to restore the balance in the energy flow.

So how do you sense chakras? Well, to begin with, it is easier to sense chakras on another person compared to sensing chakras on yourself.

First, you need to have a basic idea of exactly where the chakras are located and how you can visualize them.

1. The root chakra is the first chakra, and it is present at the base of your spine. Think of it as a red wheel of energy.

2. The sacral chakra is present in your lower abdomen, and you can visualize it as an orange wheel of energy.

3. The solar plexus chakra is present between your navel and the base of your sternum in the upper abdomen. It can be visualized like a yellow energy wheel.

4. The heart chakra lies in the center of your chest at the same level as your heart. It is a green wheel of energy.

5. The throat chakra is present in your throat and can be visualized as a light blue wheel of energy.

6. The third eye chakra is present a little above and between your eyebrows. Think of it as an indigo-colored energy wheel.

7. The crown chakra is the last chakra and is present at the top of your head. It is usually linked to the color violet or white.

Using Hands to Sense Chakras

Let us look at how you can sense chakras on a person using your hands:

Let the person lie down on a bed or a massage table. Get them comfortable before you begin your Reiki session. Now hold up your hands a little above their body. Start moving your hands slowly along the central channel. Begin from the location of the first chakra until you reach the crown chakra. As you move your hands, notice if you feel any sensations as they pass over each chakra. Experiencing sensations with your hands is more common than seeing images or colors while conducting this exercise. It is a highly individual experience.

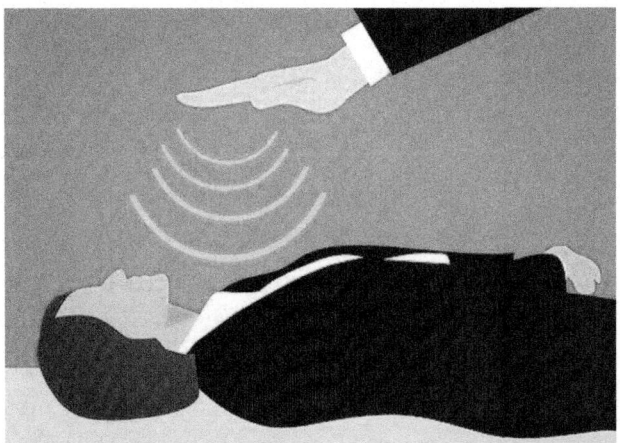

https://pixabay.com/sv/illustrations/energil%C3%A4kning-helande-h%C3%A4nder-l%C3%A4kning-3182787/

When healers start practicing this, they usually begin by sensing some subtle energy. This could happen in the form of warmth or a buzzing in the hands. However, with more experience, energy sensitivity increases as well. As you do this and sense the chakras, you will slowly become more attuned to the energy activity in each chakra. Healers with more experience will tell when there is some imbalance in a chakra. The characteristics of the energy over each chakra may differ. You might experience a difference in the intensity of the energy or variations in other qualities. What each healer experiences can be completely different from that experienced by others. Do not worry if you don't feel anything; in such cases, use your imagination, and this will allow you to unblock your ability to perceive energy over time. When you think that you are feeling something, it is probably an energy sensation. Trust in your experience and keep practicing. Over time, your energy sensitivity will increase.

Exercises

Sensing Energy

Sensing energy is an ability you are innately born with, but it requires practice for you to use this ability. There is no specific organ in the body that does this energy sensing. If you open your mind and focus, you can sense energy. There is energy present everywhere around you and inside you. Sensing the energy within your body is easier at first. To do this, you simply have to begin by feeling your body.

You may not have any direct experience working with energy, so begin by touching the surface of your body using your hands. This is the most basic way to feel your body. Another way is by increasing your awareness. This will allow you to feel the body from within. For this, you have to use your mind to focus on the specific part of the body.

As a beginner, it is easiest to start working with your hands as they are more sensitive to subtle shifts in energy than any other part of your anatomy.

Meditation Exercise for Sensing Energy

- Keeping your back straight, stand or sit according to your preference.
- Now, bring your hands out in front of your chest and keep two inches of space between them as you turn your palms toward each other.
- Now, with a calm mind, focus all your attention on your palms and the two inches of space between them.
- Take a deep breath in and move your palms away from each other.
- Then exhale and bring your palms back toward each other.
- Continue this inward and outward motion with your palms and focus your mind. You will sense energy in the form

of tingling, cold, heat, electricity, stickiness, pressure, or lightness. All of these are energy sensations.

- After doing this for a few minutes, slowly lower your hands back to the ground. Take three breaths in and out.

Using this meditation, your energy-sensing ability can be honed over time. The more you increase your awareness, the easier it gets to sense energy. It will also help you expand the area of your focus from one single point to the entire body. After a while, you will sense the energy that surrounds your body, the environment around you, and the energy that comes from other people or objects.

A heightened ability to sense energy helps you to understand the state of the energy to improve it. Being energy sensitive will also allow you to access much more information, which helps you make better decisions in life.

Creating an Energy Ball

So, what is an energy ball, and how can you create one?

Have you ever felt like you need a boost of energy? Do you want to get better at manifesting and be able to do it quickly? Well, today, you will learn how to do this with an energy ball.

You may have heard of a chi ball, and this is exactly what an energy ball is. Chi is a term used for life force energy. With a chi ball or an energy ball, you can connect with the energy of the powerful force of life and the universe. This will then allow you to use the energy positively.

Learning to make an energy ball will allow you to use it when you want to give yourself or someone else some positive energy. It can be used in many ways:

- To re-energize when you feel fatigued or exhausted.
- To feel better when you are under the weather.
- To heal your pet when they feel unwell.
- To add a layer of protection around yourself.
- To manifest what you want on a particular day.

Creating an energy ball means creating an energy field within your hands. Energy is pulled into your hands like catching a ball, and the power from this ball of energy can then be harnessed. This energy can be applied to any area you want.

If you think about it, you will realize that you have already sensed energy with your hands. For instance, you might have felt a certain way after shaking someone's hand. They might make you feel uncomfortable, or they might give off warmth that makes you trust them. Even when someone touches your arm to comfort you, you might have felt the energy of their love toward you. When someone hugs you, it allows you to receive loving energy from their heart chakra as well as their hand chakra.

Hand Chakras

There is a chakra in the palm of each of your hands. These chakras are wheels of energy that can receive and release energy. Your hand chakras will help your manifest creativity, openness, and confidence. When you open these chakras, you open yourself up to many things. You become more receptive toward compliments, and your self-worth gets boosted. You start celebrating your talents and gifts. You are more open to debating rather than arguing with people. It gives you the ability to be more sensitive to situations. Like any other chakra in the body, your hand chakras may be overactive, blocked, or underactive. This is why it is important to learn to keep a healthy flow of uninterrupted energy going through them.

Exercise

- Take a deep breath in, and then let it out. Do this a few times. Now visualize a white light coming from your crown area and filling you with energy.
- Center yourself with your heart chakra and push the energy from there into the earth. Then visualize a golden stream of light coming up from the earth through your feet into your body. Visualize this golden energy opening and

activating every chakra as it moves up your body. As it does this, it moves out from the top of your head and connects with the white light again.

- Now visualize all the energy from all your chakras moving toward your palms and finding an exit.

- Bring your palms together in front of you and then rub them together a little. Slowly pull your palms away from each other and focus on how you feel. You might experience a pulling sensation in the space between your palms. As you bring the palms closer to each other, you might experience some resistance. This is the energy created through exercise.

- Keep pulling your palms inward and outward until you feel like a ball of energy is present between them. You will feel like a real energy ball lies between your hands.

During this exercise, you might feel some tingling in your fingertips or your palms. You may also feel them shake. There may be a hot or cold sensation coming from your palms, too. While some people can see the energy ball, it is more important for you to feel it.

Keep playing around with the energy in your hands until you feel like you really have an energy ball. It may take practice, but you will soon create such energy balls for Reiki. When you feel like an energy ball is ready during an exercise, it can be used for healing. The ball of energy can be directed toward the area of healing. For instance, if you or someone else has a stomachache, you can direct the energy ball toward that specific area to promote healing.

Healers will instinctively tell when the healing process is completed. When you feel this, just rub your hands together and away from each other. This allows you to release the energy from your hands. Do not hold energy in your hands after the healing and, more importantly, don't absorb energy from someone else and hold it in your body.

Opening the Chakras

The chakras in the body contribute to a person's well-being. When the chakras are open and active, with a steady flow of energy going through, a person is in optimal health. However, most of us have some chakras that are closed, half-open, overactive, or underactive at some point or another. When this happens, there is a lack of balance in our systems.

To be healed and to heal someone else with Reiki, you must open your chakras or theirs and restore the balance. When you want to open your chakras, you do not have to focus on any overactive chakras. This excessive activity usually occurs to make up for the inactivity in the chakra that is closed. When you open the closed chakra, the overactive chakra will stop compensating for it, and the energy flow will be balanced again.

Opening the Root Chakra

The root chakra is connected to physical awareness and being comfortable in situations. When this chakra is open, you will feel stable, secure, sensible, and balanced. If it is closed, you'll feel yourself constantly mistrusting people and finding it difficult to be present. On opening the chakra, you should feel a deeper connection with your physical body and the present.

When this chakra is underactive, it will make you nervous or fearful. You will often feel unwelcome around people. When this chakra is overactive, you will act greedily and materialistically. You will not be open to any changes and constantly seek security. To avoid these feelings and open your chakra, you need to move—take a walk around a park, do some yoga, or just clean your house. These activities will make you aware of your body and strengthen the root chakra. Ground yourself. Stand straight but in a relaxed way. Keep your feet apart at a shoulder-width distance and bend your knees a little. Then move the pelvis a little forward while balancing your body.

Your weight should feel evenly distributed over your feet. Now sink this weight forward. Keep your body positioned like this for a couple of minutes.

Once you ground yourself, lower yourself down to a cross-legged sitting position. Place your hands over each knee and palms turned upward. Touch the tips of your index finger with your thumb tips. Then focus on the root chakra and its significance. Visualize this chakra as it lies between the anus and the genitals. Use the sound "LAM" to chant clearly.

While doing this, relax while you think of the chakra and what it means in your life. Think of how you want the chakra to affect your life. Visualize a red flower that is closed. Imagine powerful energy being radiated from this flower as the petals slowly open. Holding your breath, contract your perineum, and release.

Opening the Sacral Chakra

The sacral chakra is linked to sexuality and feeling. When this chakra is open, your feelings will be released liberally, and you can express yourself without feeling overemotional. You will be outgoing and passionate. It will also ensure that you have no issues with sexuality. When this chakra is underactive, it will cause you to be impassive or unemotional. You will not open up easily to anyone around you. When this chakra is overactive, you'll be too emotional and sensitive most of the time. It will also increase your sexual needs.

Get down on your knees and sit with an upright back. Be relaxed. Place one hand over the other and lay them on your lap. Both palms should be turned upward. The right hand should lie over the left hand. The palm of your left hand should be touching the fingers of your right hand with the thumbs gently touching as well. Now place your concentration on where the sacral chakra lies near the sacral bone and think of what it signifies. Use the sound "VAM" to start clearly yet silently chanting.

While you do this, be relaxed as you think of the significance of the sacral chakra. Think of how you want this chakra to work in your life. Repeat all of this until you feel completely relaxed and cleansed.

Opening the Navel Chakra

This chakra is linked to confidence. When the chakra is open, you will feel like you are in control and dignified. When the chakra is underactive, you'll be indecisive and act passively. It will make you constantly apprehensive. When it is overactive, the chakra will make you aggressive and imperious. Get down on your knees and be relaxed. Your back should be straight but not stiff. Place your hands in front of you, in front of your stomach. This is a little below where the solar plexus lies. Join your hands together in a prayer-like hand position but with your fingers facing away from you. Keep your fingers straight and cross your thumbs. Now focus on your navel chakra and meditate on what it signifies.

The chakra is present a little above your navel toward your spine. Start chanting the word "RAM" clearly yet silently. Try and relax while you do this but keep concentrating on the chakra. Think of how it currently affects your life and how you want it to be. Keep repeating this until you feel like your chakra is cleansed and stable.

Opening the Heart Chakra

The heart chakra is linked to love, endearment, and caring. If the chakra is open, it will make you friendly and compassionate. You will always have amicable relationships with the people around you. When it is underactive, you'll be unfriendly and cold. When the chakra is overactive, you will act more lovingly than people would want you to. This kind of love and care often seems to smother others, and they will see you as a selfish person. Sit down in a cross-legged position. Place each hand over each knee with the palms facing upward.

Touch the tips of your thumbs with your index fingers. Then move your right hand up to your chest. Hold it a little below the lower half of your breastbone. Now focus on the heart chakra present at the level of your heart in the spine. Use the word "YAM" to clearly yet silently chant. Try to relax while you do this. Think of the chakra and its significance. Think of how you want the heart chakra to impact your life. Repeat this exercise until you feel cleansed.

Opening the Throat Chakra

This chakra is linked to communication and self-expression. If the throat chakra is open, you will find it easy to express yourself. Art will seem like a great medium for self-expression. When the chakra is underactive, you'll seem like a shy person to others since you will not speak too much. This chakra is probably blocked if you find yourself lying too often. When it is overactive, you talk too much and annoy the people around you, and you stop being a good listener. Get down on your knees and sit.

Join the fingers of both hands with every finger other than your thumbs crossed. Your thumbs should be lying upward and touching at the tips. Now start thinking of the throat chakra and its significance. The chakra is present at the base of your throat. Chant the word "HAM" silently to yourself. Relax as you chant and think of the meaning of this chakra. Repeat this exercise for a few minutes until you feel intensely cleansed.

Opening the Third Eye Chakra

This chakra is linked to insight. If the third eye chakra is open, you have many dreams and will experience clairvoyance. When it is underactive, you will depend on other people to make decisions and think for you. You will be confused most of the time and rely on beliefs too much. When the chakra is overactive, you will tend to daydream too much. You might even start hallucinating when this happens in extremes. Sit down in a cross-legged position. Bring your hands together in front of the lower half of your breast.

The tips of your middle fingers should touch each other as they point away from you. Bend your other fingers and keep them touching at the upper two phalanges. Your thumbs should meet at the top and point at you. Now start focusing on your third eye chakra, which is present just above the middle of both your eyebrows. Use the word "AUM" or "OM" to start chanting silently. Try and relax while you do all this and keep concentrating on the third eye chakra. Think of how the chakra affects your life, its significance, and how you want it to function. Repeat this until you feel intensely cleansed.

Opening the Crown Chakra

The crown chakra is extremely spiritual. It is linked to wisdom and is a person's link to the universe. If the chakra is open, you will be much more aware of yourself and the world around you. You will not be prejudiced in any way. When the chakra is underactive, you will be more rigid in your thinking and less spiritual. When it is overactive, you will constantly try to intellectualize things.

The first thing that will come to your mind is spirituality, and in extremes, it may even make you ignore your basic worldly needs like shelter and food. Sit down in a cross-legged position. Place your hands together over your stomach. Keep the little fingers pointed away from you and upward as they touch at the tips. The right thumb should lie above the left thumb. The rest of your fingers should be crossed. Now focus on your crown chakra and its significance.

Visualize it as it lies at the top of your head. Silently chant the sound "NF." Your body should be relaxed and your mind at peace. Keep concentrating on the chakra. Meditating on this chakra takes longer than others. Repeat the exercise for ten minutes at the very least. Another thing to keep in mind is that you should not meditate on the crown chakra until your root chakra is open and strong. Having a strong foundation is essential before meditating on the crown chakra.

Chapter 4: Psychic Abilities in Healing

While meditation and sensing energies are helpful, it also helps to have some psychic abilities, such as clairvoyance and clairsentience. When healing someone with Reiki, messages and visions tend to come through, which assist with the healing process and/or need to be transferred to the patient. Here you will learn how psychic abilities may be useful in Reiki healing. There are exercises that you can implement to develop your psychic abilities as well.

Regardless of your stance on psychics and psychic powers, every person has a unique intuition and way of learning and manifesting psychic abilities. In fact, according to some of the most well-known psychics, every one of us possesses that otherworldly sense, and all we need to do is focus on it and keep learning how to develop our psychic abilities. Psychic powers and "intuition" are very similar, and they are often used interchangeably.

In addition, we all possess an otherworldly sense, and the ability to tap into that power can also reflect on our ability to feel, see, and hear things beyond the physical realm and help us delve into the psychic realm. This might happen daily, both knowingly and unknowingly.

Still having a hard time being convinced? Think about this: have you ever felt like someone is staring at you and turned around to find someone is staring at you? Do you really believe that this thought popped into your mind randomly, or is there something more to it than meets the eye? Have you ever felt certain energy when you walk into a room without even knowing anything about the people who might be inside the room? All of these can be looked at as random thoughts that come up in your mind. They can also be seen as some of the best examples of the intuitive psychic gift we all possess.

Akin to any gift or ability, we can reactivate and hone these psychic abilities to become brighter, stronger, and more vibrant versions of ourselves. It can become a very practical and incredibly powerful tool for us, which can help us navigate through the journey of life in different areas, whether in our relationships, our career paths, artistic abilities, or whatever else that may be important to us.

To add to these positive benefits, when you make a conscious decision to harness your intuitive abilities, it affects your life and creates a positive chain reaction that enhances and improves the intuitive powers of the people who are part of your life. If that is enough to convince you to begin the journey of amping up your intuitive dial, it is now time to look at some of the ways to develop and hone your psychic abilities.

Developing Your Psychic Abilities

Be Open to the Possibility of Tapping into Your Psychic Skills

The first and foremost thing that inhibits a person's journey into developing and exploring their psychic and intuitive abilities is their fear or close-mindedness toward the subject at hand. According to most psychic experts, most people are afraid of their natural psychic abilities, especially because of the potential negative consequences that might come with the experience. It is important to understand that these things are not something to fear.

These natural psychic abilities have always been within us to help lead us toward our highest potential. They act as navigational tools for us to travel through the journey of life. The first step toward developing your psychic skills is the simple act of being willing and open to tapping into your psychic abilities. Without believing in yourself, almost nothing is successful. Experts suggest that making a declaration to the universe stating that you are open and ready to explore these psychic gifts is useful. This can help you stop the fear and open your mind to the brighter possibilities these otherworldly activities can bring.

Learn to Read People's Energies

Have you ever noticed how some people give off a very bad "vibe" or energy for no concrete reason? This is not something that your mind simply concocts without any reason; rather, it is your psychic intuition coming through. This is what "reading someone's energy" means, and it is a skill you can develop and strengthen with time and practice. One way of doing this is by constantly challenging yourself to read and interpret people's energy, seeing beyond their facades and what they say, and tuning into their vibes.

Although that may sound very abstract, and you may be wondering how one reads people's energies, it is much simpler than you might think. Simply spending time with the person is a good place to start. Doing this allows you to learn your thoughts and feelings about that person, and how these feelings reflect on that person is a great way of reading their energy.

According to many experts, reading a person's energy is possible even before directly talking or interacting with them. For instance, if you are waiting in line at the grocery store, you can tap into the energy of the person behind you or in front of you and see what comes up in your mind. If it feels positive, strike up a conversation with them to find out whether your intuition was correct or you misjudged the person. It takes some time and practice before you start reading people correctly.

Develop a Connection with Your Spirit Guides

A spirit guide is a subject that many people are skeptical about and is often frowned upon, particularly by people who are not familiar with the subject. As individuals with intuition and psychic abilities, spirit guides are something that we can all call on to garner mental and emotional support. Spirit guides can be looked at as unique and advanced soul mentors in the angelic realm and help us by guiding and teaching us things that we may normally not be capable of.

Most professional psychics believe that we are also connected to anyone close whom we may have lost and who may have crossed to the "other side." One of the most common ways of identifying and finding your spirit guide is by asking for very specific signs from the universe. For instance, if you are at the crossroads of making a very important decision and you need confirmation to know that you are on the right track, you can ask for a sign from the universe by requesting something as strange as seeing a pink panther.

The best results come about when you get specific with your requests while asking for a sign, so when you actually do receive a sign from the universe, there is absolutely no denying that it is a sign from your spirit guides and not just another random occurrence.

Communicating with your spirit guides gets easier if you do it daily. If you have not been talking to your spirit guides, there is not much to worry about because it is much easier than most people think. The only thing you need to do is simply check in with your spirit guides throughout the day. It's important to take notice of any visualizations or intuitive nudges that might come to mind after communicating with your spirit guide.

Begin Predicting How Places Appear

Reading and interpreting someone's energy is not the only way to develop your psychic intuition. To develop a well-rounded psyche, you can also practice "psychic seeing," more popularly known as "clairvoyance."

Most experts recommended practicing remote-viewing exercises. For instance, the next time you are planning to go somewhere that you have never visited, like a new restaurant, sometime ahead of your actual visit, close your eyes and "declare" what you want to see in that location.

Draw a rudimentary depiction of your vision on a piece of paper regardless of what comes up. When you visit the location later, you can compare your drawing to what the place really looks like. You may find many similarities between what you envisioned and what you see, and sometimes the similarities can be very specific. For instance, the location of a window or the exact type of potted plants you previously envisioned while practicing clairvoyance may be present.

Exercises That Help You Develop Clairvoyance

Visualization

Visualization is a form of exercise meant to enhance a specific part of you, akin to working out or practicing yoga (which is meant to enhance your physical attributes). Visualization can help strengthen and fine-tune the third-eye muscles present in your brain. The best part about this technique is that you can do this exercise using almost anything.

Many people prefer using flowers (you can even use real flowers to make the experience more engaging and interactive). Start the exercise by placing a flower in front of you and staring at it, trying to keep any thoughts out of your mind, other than the flower. Next, close your eyes and visualize the flower with as much detail as you possibly can.

Visualize different aspects of the flower, such as its color, shape, and size. Flood your mind with these details as accurately as you can. Practicing these clairvoyant exercises regularly will help you develop and hone your psychic abilities.

Daydreaming

Although many people may have a different opinion when it comes to daydreaming, a big part of clairvoyance is the ability to visualize things in your mind. Try strolling down memory lane and remember those childhood days while letting your logical mind take a back seat and relax for a while. Try to free your mind from the cacophony of thoughts that usually bombard your psyche and close your eyes.

Focus on your forehead, specifically on the area between your eyebrows or the "third eye" area. Try communicating with your spirit guides and make a request for them to show you peaceful and beautiful images. Avoid trying to control your visualizations or overthinking what you are currently visualizing. Allow your mind to wander, and let your spirit guides connect with your inner self through clairvoyance.

Setting Intentions

Once you have finished becoming acquainted with your spirit guides, practicing clairvoyant exercises becomes much easier and more comforting. Intuitive gifts such as clairvoyance, clairaudience, claircognizance, and clairsentience are the primary ways spirit guides communicate with you, and the better you are at communicating with them, the more they will let you in.

If you feel like you are in a stagnant state of mind, indecisive, and unsure of what to do first, ask your spirit guides for guidance. Setting the right intentions in your life and asking for divine guidance from your spirit guides can change your life. Once you have finished setting the right intentions in life, you should look for the signs that your spirit guides provide you with.

Seeing Auras

Contrary to popular belief, auras are real, and anybody can detect them. An aura can be best described as a field of energy that surrounds all living creatures. For a start, you can practice seeing auras by asking a friend to stand in front of a solid-colored surface or wall.

Stand back about eight feet (stand back enough so that you can see them from head to toe without having to look up or down).

Try focusing on the center of your friend's forehead (the third eye) and visualize yourself looking through their physical body. Gradually you will start noticing a bright area around their head. Voila! You have successfully seen their aura. Regular practice will make the process easier.

Meet Other Mediums and Psychics

Being a psychic healer or Reiki healer is a unique career path. There are certain obstacles and challenges that people who choose this career path face—the rest of the world will never understand you or get what you do. The journey becomes much easier and more rewarding if you have the support of people who understand what you do and the challenges you face. They can also give you some useful pointers and serve as excellent practice partners for you to develop and sharpen your skills.

Learn How to Turn Your Gifts "ON" and "OFF"

Once you have successfully developed your gift of clairvoyance, the next thing that you will want to do is to learn how to control it as and when the need arises. It is important to turn it "ON" only when you need to and let go when you need to tune out of things. Prior to practicing any exercises related to clairvoyance, start with the simple ritual of visualizing the act of lighting a candle within your mind. While you are doing so, invite your spirit guides, and you will get a feeling that your gifts have turned on. This candle visualization exercise will let your spirit guides and spiritual helpers offer you divine support and elevate your intuition and spiritual communicative skills.

Learning to turn off your clairvoyant and psychic intuition is another thing that you will need to learn as you develop your skills. Like turning it ON, imagine blowing out the candle once you have finished practicing. Once you have wrapped everything up, imagine blowing out the candle in your mind and making sure that you pay gratitude to your spiritual helpers for their divine support. Doing this can help you harness your gifts and control them when you are not working with them or have finished any healing or given a psychic reading to a client.

Maintain a Journal

Once you have begun developing a connection with your spirit guides as well as your "higher self," you will want to jot down the important things that you notice and the changes that manifest after you have begun to become more intuitive. Many experts believe that if meditation is chocolate, journaling is peanut butter. Writing down important thoughts, intentions and manifestations can help you get in touch with your higher self and spirit guides, thereby improving your intuition and clairvoyance.

For instance, think of the moments in life where you were immensely happy and grateful. It could be anything from a near-death experience to a loved one visiting unexpectedly. It can be something groundbreaking, or it can be something as simple as staying in for the weekend with your partner and having an intimate experience with them.

Jot down how you were feeling at the time and how that experience stayed with you and changed you in the days that followed. It can help you relive those important moments that helped you take your intuition and psyche to another level without forgetting the important details. Journaling can also be a very good activity to engage in after a meditation session when the mind is in a calm and relaxed state. It will help you maintain good energy and raise your "vibrations."

Develop Healthy Food Habits

The food you eat makes you what you are and affects your intuition and vibrations. Eating healthy foods does not necessarily mean only eating leafy greens or salads for every single meal. Incorporating high vibrational foods into your everyday diet, such as fresh fruit, dark chocolate, whole foods, and removing highly processed food products can help you develop a stronger aura and raise your energetic vibe. Eating healthier foods also helps you feel better physically, thereby making it easier to develop your intuition and psychic abilities.

Activate Your Third Eye

The third eye or the pineal gland is widely considered the seat of psychic intelligence and clairvoyance and is regularly mentioned in Eastern Mysticism and Egyptian history. The third eye works like a muscle. The more you use it and flex it, the stronger it becomes. Activating the third eye is not a complicated task; it is quite easy. For starters, place your index finger on the third eye (the region between your eyebrows) and gently tap on the area a few times and imagine that it is opening. Feeling a tingling sensation in that area is normal as it means that your clairvoyance is getting activated. Repeat this practice regularly, and you will begin noticing some important changes in your psyche and clairvoyance. If you are having trouble activating your third eye, you can join a spiritual development circle or take special classes where more experienced individuals who have already gone through this process can give you spiritual guidance and help you activate your third eye in a safe and loving environment.

https://pixabay.com/sv/photos/tredje-%C3%B6gat-%C3%B6ga-andlig-intuition-2886688/

Strengthen Your Third Eye

Even though this may be the last thing on the list, it is probably the most important practice that you should engage in regularly. The third eye is the seat of all psychic abilities and where your clairvoyance stems from. As you hone and develop your psychic abilities, you must learn to trust them. You should be able to trust the visualizations and intuitive images that come to your mind when practicing healing rituals and psychic readings. You should regularly practice meditation and self-reflective techniques that will activate and enhance your abilities. Use crystals such as fluorite and moonstone and place them on your third eye to draw energy from the crystals and strengthen your psychic capabilities and clairvoyance.

Chapter 5: The Reiki Method

A Brief History of Reiki

Although there have been numerous attempts at explaining the history of Reiki, unfortunately, most of these explanations are based on mysticism and the actual need to validate a particular form of Reiki. Most of these explanations lack verified information. Therefore, to work on a fact-based outlook, let us dig deeper into the field of Reiki and try to explain what it really is.

Mikao Usui or Usui Sensei Is Considered by Many People to Have Been the Creator of Reiki

Usui's version of Reiki applied only to the different healing methodologies he was responsible for discovering and developing. When researching the facts about the origin of Reiki, we find that before the rise in popularity of Usui's Reiki methods, Reiki healing was practiced in Japan in four different ways.

Most of these snippets of information come from two Japanese Reiki researchers: Toshitaka Mochitzuki Sensei and Hiroshi Doi Sensei. After the era of Usui Reiki, a Japanese therapist named Matji Kawakami came up with a different style of Reiki healing known as Reiki Ryoho in 1919, details of which can be found in his publication entitled *Reiki Ryoho to Sono Koka* or *Reiki Healing and Its Effects*.

The other styles prevalent were Senshinryu Reiki Ryoho by Kogetsu Matsubara, Reikan Tonetsu Ryoho by Reikaku Ishinuki, and Seido Reisho Jitsu by Reisen Oyama.

Although there are different opinions on what should or should not be called Reiki, we must consider that there are many different styles and disciplines of Reiki healing that have their lineage going back to Usui Reiki. It is considered a form of energy that anyone can use, and many have done so over time. It is safe to say that any healing methodology that applies Reiki energy can be called Reiki and not just those modalities defined by Usui Sensei.

The Essence of Reiki

When we focus on Reiki energy for any purpose—be it healing, teaching, or giving attunements to your clients—especially while using Fire Reiki for placements and ignitions, one becomes more and more aware of a wealth of positivity and good qualities that Reiki energy embodies.

The positive qualities transcend the different states of consciousness that we are usually aware of, and Reiki energy can elevate us into transcendental levels of joy, happiness, and peace. In addition, these qualities are also helpful for individuals to develop healthy and positive traits as a part of their personalities. Since all Reiki modalities respect free will, none of these modalities will help us heal or transcend into a higher state of mind unless we are open to it and invite it to do so. This means that Reiki's healing methods are only effective if we are willing to change.

A person's ability to identify flaws and unhealthy personal qualities within themselves and their willingness to let them go is of utmost importance if they want to move forward with their personal healing and mental development. The Reiki process can involve anything that might help improve the overall quality of Reiki energy that a person can channel or imbibe and develop the qualities considered healthy for a person to possess.

Some of the positive and healthy character traits that Reiki can develop and elevate include patience, compassion, non-competitiveness, self-love, and love for others. It takes us to a place of acceptance of others' ideas and beliefs, and it also helps us become accepting and non-judgmental, empowering our ability to forgive others and develop gratitude for all the wonderful things we have experienced and are blessed with, such as friends and family. This alone can significantly improve the quality of joy and peace we experience in life and, most importantly, it increases our ability to channel the source of Reiki energy into an everlasting and strong feeling of security that embodies all Reiki modalities.

Understanding this is what will eventually help you to appreciate Reiki healing and its unlimited potential. This idea is clearly validated by the fact that most sensei of Reiki, including Usui Sensei and Hayashi Sensei, encouraged all their students to work on improving and refining the quality of Reiki energy that they were capable of channeling. It is also very clear from the concept that if Reiki is a form of unlimited potential, as most people will agree it is, then no matter how good and effective you are at channeling Reiki energy, it is always possible for you to become better and more effective at it.

Just receiving the attunement and ignition does not give you complete access to Reiki energy, but it does mean that you are able to channel Reiki energy to a certain degree, and if you can work further on that aspect, your ability to channel a higher and more refined form of energy becomes more and more effective. This aspect of self-awareness becomes clearer when you practice Holy Fire Reiki as you begin to experience an even higher level of peace, joy, and love, and it will show you how wonderful and important it is to incorporate Reiki energy into your everyday life.

Benefits of Reiki Healing

Reiki is an ancient and simple healing technique touting some profound benefits all through the art of gentle touch, having a positive mindset, and the transfer of positive energy. Whether you are adopting Reiki to treat emotional trauma, spiritual, and emotional development, or to balance your energy levels, Reiki has endless advantages. Let us look at some of the benefits that Reiki healing may bring about.

It is important to keep in mind that Reiki does not target one single aspect of the body and instead targets the whole body at once. The transfer of positive energy is one of the most powerful tools for healing the body and mind, and that is how Reiki is effective in healing all related elements of any bodily or mental condition instead of only targeting that condition.

Promoting Balance and Harmony

Reiki healing adopts a very non-invasive approach to the transfer of energy. Through this energy transfer, your body can restore balance throughout all the different systems of the mind, body, and spirit. This creates a balance and harmony within you and helps you to continue leading a positive lifestyle.

Improves Focus and Mental Clarity

Reiki methodologies remind receivers to be present in the moment instead of being stuck in the past or worrying about the future. The energy transfer allows the mind to focus on the present moment and not hold onto past mistakes or be constantly anxious about the future. This helps individuals become more accepting about the uncertain nature of life and will help one promote positive reactions to different circumstances, people, situations, and surprises that life might have in store for them.

Alleviates and Eradicates Tension from the Body

The most attractive aspect of Reiki is the idea to simply "be." The process of Reiki healing is best described as a few minutes of complete relaxation where the person receiving the energy can rid their mind of anxiety and stress. The transfer of energy through Reiki can make people feel relaxed and somehow lighter, which helps them get in touch with their inner self and promote self-reflect in their lives.

Gets Rid of Energy Blocks and Balances the Mind, Body, and Spirit

Regular Reiki treatment promotes the consistent flow of energy throughout the body by removing any energy blocks that may be restricting or aggravating the flow of energy between the different chakras of the body. Doing this releases the mind from stress, enhances memory and learning abilities, and promotes mental clarity and physical recovery.

When the pathways that allow the flow of energy are blocked due to stress or trauma, positive energy is restricted from flowing into certain parts of the body—depending upon where the blockage is present. This results in mood swings, anger, fear, insecurity, and pain. Reiki healing practices can help you remove these energy blocks and keep these energy pathways clear.

Gets Rid of Toxins and Improves the Immune Systems

Many Reiki healing techniques are also used to initiate recovery by reminding our bodies to get into a mode of "self-repair" or "self-healing," improving your ability to rest, recover, and digest food. By triggering the body and mind to initiate this state, our bodies begin to eliminate the negative energies and toxins that might otherwise be causing trouble or discomfort. It also helps the body protect itself from disease, exhaustion, and burnout and prevents the immune system from becoming compromised.

Improves the Quality of Sleep

Reiki sessions are extremely relaxing, and that kind of relaxation can help your body sleep better, have more mental clarity, and heal better. Do not be surprised or disappointed if you fall asleep during a Reiki session, as that is a common occurrence for many people.

Accelerates the Self-Healing Ability of the Body

Reiki energy can improve the different bodily systems, including breathing, heart rate, circulation, blood pressure, and hormone levels. This balanced state of the body will help it to heal from within.

Promotes Emotional Cleansing and Spiritual Growth

When positive energy is transferred through the different parts of the mind and body, it helps elevate the receiver's mood and improves their general perspective on life. These positive changes start from within a person, which is reflected in the decisions they make and the perspective they might have on the outside.

Reiki Methods

Clearing the Space with Reiki

The positive Reiki energy that flows through your body during a Reiki session can also flow through your living space or your workspace and, in doing this, can have profound beneficial effects. Moreover, the Reiki therapy that you perform on yourself or other people will be enhanced significantly if your space has also been cleared with the help of Reiki energy.

Other than your energy, the energy emanating from the Earth and its magnetic field can also affect the balance of your living space or working space. Some of the most common sources of discomfort can be perceived using electronic devices, whereas others are subtler and need a keener sense of intuition to detect. Space clearing can be done using many different mediums, such as essential oils, incense/sage, or different types of crystals.

Doing this can be transformative and help significantly boost the effectiveness of anything that you might be engaged in. Whatever method you choose to adopt should be treated as something sacred.

Centering

Before you start your Reiki session, you will need to center yourself. Gassho is one of the most common ways of centering yourself—this is where one places both hands in a prayer position with the thumbs placed against the breastbone. Lower your head or bow down so that your chin rests directly on top of the middle fingers of your hands. While seated or standing in this position, focus on your palm chakras and feel your breath moving over your hands.

While doing this, it is natural for some strange thoughts to wander into your mind. The best thing to do here is to recognize these thoughts and let them pass instead of trying to ignore them altogether. This is the building block of any meditation technique. Gassho can be practiced between twenty and thirty minutes every day to clear the mind and help you focus on the actual Reiki session.

From this position, slowly move your hands until your thumbs are at the center of the third eye to increase your intuitive powers. While you are in this position, you should try to communicate with your inner intentions and direct yourself to the Reiki practice while setting aside your logical mind for the time being. Focus your mind on the palm chakras as you feel the flow of Reiki energy.

From here, move your hands slowly and place them over your navel, known as the Tanden, and let go of all the thoughts in your mind as you let the positive Reiki energy flow through your body. The Tanden is also known as the location of your center, and when you have directed your focus toward your center, you will feel a balance and harmony within your body and mind.

Using the Reiki Box

A Reiki box is just what the name suggests it is. It's a box used to contain or channel an infinite reservoir of energy into a specified space to fulfill a certain purpose. The basis of the Reiki box is that Reiki energy itself is sufficient to manifest whatever we need for our specific intentions or missions. Since it is easier for us to work with something concrete and tangible, working with the Reiki box will help you achieve this. The box can heal using different aspects of Reiki healing and manifestation, and it can also be used to send positive Reiki energy across distances to multiple subjects simultaneously.

Basic Procedure

Reiki is one of the best energy-healing techniques where an experienced practitioner of Reiki who is properly attuned can channel this positive life force into those in dire need of it. The best part about it is that it becomes possible to send Reiki energy across long distances.

Let us look at one of the most basic and common techniques used to achieve good results during healing. When implemented correctly, you are bound to receive positive benefits, maintain equilibrium in the body or mind, and prosper in life.

Using the Reiki Box

1. Find a simple box made from eco-friendly materials.

2. Make sure that you clean the box before using it to house the most positive Reiki energy.

3. Draw the Reiki power symbol on the box—be it on the walls, base, or lid. If you are properly attuned, you can also draw the Reiki master symbol.

4. Place the box between your palms and steadily direct the Reiki energy into it. If you are new to the practice of Reiki, you can skip over the previous step.

5. Use paper to prepare the intention slips—pieces of paper containing descriptions of your healing requests or deepest desires.

6. Most experienced Reiki masters recommend writing these intentions in the present tense as if these intentions have already manifested.

7. Draw the Reiki symbols on each of the intention slips and place them into the Reiki box. Close the box.

8. Repeat the process of channeling Reiki energy into the box for a few minutes every day. Make sure that you store the box in a private and safe space.

9. Keep checking the intention slips periodically to track your progress and discard the intention slips whose purpose has already been served. Make sure that you are grateful while discarding these slips.

10. Repeat the entire process.

Chapter 6: Scanning the Aura

A Reiki session begins by identifying imbalances in the energy and auric field of the person receiving treatment. You will learn how you can sense your auric imbalances and identify such imbalances in others. You will also learn what the colors of the aura mean and what physical/mental/emotional conditions they indicate.

A Brief History of Auras

Going back to the era of Christian Mystics of the Middle Ages, a person's aura was depicted as a light surrounding the person as portrayed by most artists and painters. Over the years, many scientists and researchers have tried to capture the human aura through photography techniques and other forms of modern technology. One of the first photographs was taken by Nikola Tesla in 1891. According to more recent ideologies, auras are depicted as colored emanations and believed to enclose all living beings. The aura is a manifestation of a person's spiritual, mental, and physical health.

Many spiritual advisors and practitioners of Reiki claim to see the vibrations and colors that constitute a person's aura.

What Is an Aura

Although many people consider an aura a strange idea, many people devote a lot of energy and time to studying the meaning of auras. If you look into the subject, you might find many mixed opinions surrounding this highly polarizing subject. For all the non-believers and skeptics, auras do exist. Whether you believe in it or not is all about how it is interpreted to you, and this is where things get murky.

As per the laws of science, all living beings have a unique energy that is characteristic of them. The energy that we are talking about is a direct reflection of our state of being. Have you ever noticed how someone's presence can instantly make you feel nervous or happy without any specific reason? This is you experiencing a reaction to different types of energy.

Scientifically speaking, an aura is an electromagnetic field surrounding the body of any living being. On a spiritual level, it is believed that auras correspond to the state of our chakras and the overall state of our consciousness. Each aura is made of seven different layers that correspond to different aspects of our health—spiritual, mental, physical, and emotional. Let us look at each aura layer:

Physical Aura Layer

The physical aura layer is connected to our overall bodily health and five senses. This layer of an aura gets depleted during the hours you are awake, and it rejuvenates when we sleep and give rest to our bodies.

Astral Aura Layer

The astral aura layer is connected to our emotional state and saves our emotional experiences and memories.

Higher Aura Layer

The higher aura layer acts as a bridge between the different aura layers. The higher layer also acts as a bridge between yours and others' well-being. This layer is where our core beliefs are formed, such as selflessness and compassion.

Lower Aura Layer

The lower aura layer is connected to logical abilities and thinking patterns. Most of our waking hours are spent in this aura. The lower layer is engaged when our minds are focused on different tasks such as working, studying, or carrying out any task at hand.

Intuitional Aura Layer

The intuitional aura layer is also known as the third eye. The intuitional aura layer allows you to gain a deeper level of awareness. An individual's sensitivity and intuition are heightened at the intuitional aura layer.

Spiritual Aura Layer

The spiritual aura layer is where you connect with other people over matters that are associated with spirituality. Your spiritual aura will grow and become stronger and brighter when you share, teach, and engage with other people on a spiritual level.

Absolute Aura Layer

The absolute aura layer is the layer that harmonizes all the different aura layers. This aura layer is where all your experiences are stored, and this layer also guides you on your life's path.

Aura Colors and Their Meanings

Every layer of the human aura is represented by a specific color. The way these auras interact with each other shows how dynamic you are mentally, spiritually, and physically. For example, some aura layers may appear brighter because the person might be experiencing more vibrant energy, whereas other aura levels may appear dull if the person is feeling sick or emotionally depleted. Also, a person's aura varies as aura colors reflect differently depending on where a person is in life.

The color of a person's aura may change throughout the day depending on their emotions, energy blockages, chakra states, and the flow of energy through the body. What you see is what is happening at that moment. Therefore, you should be very careful while reading

other people's auras. Some aura colors and their corresponding meanings are given below:
1. **Turquoise:** Naturally organized, dynamic personality.
2. **Red:** Passionate and vibrant personality.
3. **Yellow:** Joyful and intellectual.
4. **Green:** Natural healer having a strong connection with nature.
5. **Pink:** Peaceful and harmonious.
6. **Murky:** Mentally or physically ill.
7. **Blue:** Intuitive and spiritual.
8. **White:** Balanced and In Harmony.

How to "Read" Auras

Learning how to read another person's aura takes a lot of practice. It is all about detecting the energy around a person's body. You begin by focusing on the feeling a person's presence incites within you. While taking deep breaths, pay attention to the different sensations you feel in your body while you inhale and exhale. How does a person's presence make you feel? Do you feel calm, irritated, or nervous around them?

The next thing to work on is enhancing your peripheral vision. Since we primarily use our central vision most of the time, it may take a while to develop your peripheral vision. To increase your sensitivity to different types of light, a good technique is to try and focus on a singular spot for thirty-sixty seconds.

As discussed earlier, energy constitutes everything, and every living being is made of energy. Auras are a great way of knowing what the energetic state of a person is. To start seeing all the colors of someone's aura, have someone stand in front of a white wall. Make sure that you are a few feet away from them and try looking through the person to the wall behind them. With enough practice, you will begin to see a specific color outlining the person's body.

The main thing to remember is that you should not focus on the person directly and try as much as you can to use your peripheral vision to view them. You will begin to see the color and light surrounding the person. Our aura is the energy surrounding our body, and it also acts as the lens through which one can view the world. To truly read a person's aura, you need to have enough self-awareness to distinguish between your energy and someone else's. This means it is important to make sure you are aware of your aura and receptive enough to scan the energy of the other person.

Everyone has psychic abilities hidden somewhere deep within them, even though most may not know it. In fact, it is widely believed that young children and toddlers are better at reading auras than adults, which might explain why the mere presence of some people seems to upset young children for no apparent reason. While this skill may decline with age, nothing is holding us back from tapping into our psychic abilities later in life.

Reading auras takes a lot of practice and patience more than anything else. There are numerous exercises that you can try that will develop your ability to read and decipher auras. Depending on a person's talent, one may be able to see an aura, feel an aura, or even "hear" someone's aura, which varies from one person to another.

How to "Interpret" Auras

Seeing someone's aura is one thing; deciphering it is a totally different ballgame. Human beings are complex creatures, and our auras are equally complex. What we project as our aura is an interplay of many things, such as our perception, experiences, knowledge, personal biases, defense mechanisms, ego, cultural lenses and how we understand the world, views on spirituality, and other societal influences.

When you see another person's aura, you are looking at it through your aura, and you are looking at it through your beliefs, perceptions, and knowledge. Quickly jumping to conclusions and making snap judgments is not a wise thing to do, so you should avoid doing that. Learning how to use your mind, heart, and soul to make accurate readings can take a while but, do not be disheartened if you struggle initially.

After you have successfully learned how to see and interpret auras, you will see them everywhere around you, be it at the shopping mall, work, or local park.

Having a lot of information might make you feel tempted to share everything you see or learn with others. A person's aura is personal, and seeing an aura can be akin to looking inside someone's bedroom and invading their privacy. This means that you should only do it once you have their consent to do so.

Reiki and Scanning Auras

To scan another person or a client, begin the session by saying a prayer and asking for guidance to identify the specific zones where the person needs Reiki energy. The next step is to place your non-dominant hand (left hand/right hand depending on your preferences) about ten or twelve inches away from the top of your client's head.

Visualize yourself, placing your consciousness on the palm of your hand and pay close attention to how you are feeling. Move your hand closer to the top of their head at about three to four inches and slowly move your hand above the person's head and toward their feet while maintaining the same distance between your hand and your client. Make sure that you move your hands very slowly and pay attention to any changes in energy that you might be registering from your palm. If you feel any changes in the energy, that is a place where your client requires Reiki energy.

Energy changes may manifest themselves as a change in temperature, a tingling sensation, pressure, irregularities, the sensation of being pulled, minor electric shocks, and pulsations. These changes may be very small, and it may be easy for you to convince yourself that they are just a figment of your imagination. You will need to trust yourself and have faith in the process to work.

When you are in the initial stages of scanning, your sensitivity to different types of energy might not be well developed, so you need to be even more attentive while starting. As you become better versed with the practice of scanning auras, your abilities will improve, and your Reiki sessions will be more effective and profound.

Once you become very adept in the process, you may find that you can even start scanning with your eyes and easily sense where the person needs Reiki energy without having to do much. Master Reiki practitioners are known to see the negative energy that plagues distressed areas of the body.

When you encounter a negative change in the energy field or the aura of an individual, move your hand up and down around that area until you find a height at which you feel the most distress. This can be as far as several feet above the person's body, or it can be somewhere that you feel drawn to touch with your hands.

Most experts recommend that the best distance is around four or five inches away from the body. When you identify the correct distance, bring both your hands over the spot and channel positive Reiki energy into that area. Reiki energy will heal the aura and promote the proper flow of energy within the physical body, helping the organs and tissues to heal as well.

Continue channeling positive Reiki energy into the detected spot until you can sense the flow of Reiki subsiding or until that area is healed. Once you have finished the healing process, rescan the area and other areas to make sure everything is healed. If you find any other energy blockages, continue to channel Reiki until everything feels complete.

Benefits

Scanning a person's aura and healing their energy field has numerous health benefits since the root cause of most illnesses and health complications lie in the person's aura. By healing a person's aura, you will be working on treating the cause of the problem, thereby healing the problems before they manifest themselves physically or medically. Even after a health complication or a problem has developed in one's body, a person will respond to Reiki healing if the aura is rectified and improved upon.

By healing the person's energy field first, you can help the person to accept Reiki energy more readily. This will allow Prana or life force to flow through the body more readily. If you want to opt for scanning and Reiki therapy, you should go with scanning first, allowing the Reiki therapy to be more profound and effective.

As you interact with a person's aura or energy field, the two of you will develop a strong and intimate connection. You will become more aware of the different distortions in a person's aura and the problems that might be associated with their aura. With more practice and experience, you can also get more insight into their problems and how they were created in the first place. This can improve your ability to facilitate healing and help your clients to a better degree. This work should be treated as something very sacred, and you should be ever respectful of the client and the process. Only with kindness and the absence of judgment can you do something positive for the people you want to help.

How to "Feel" Auras

If you are more of a sensitive person or a kinesthetic, feeling auras will be easier for you than seeing them. In the psychic world, this ability is known as clairsentience (i.e., the ability to feel things beyond the material realm). When feeling auras, the hands are the easiest tool to feel subtle energy changes and inconsistencies in a person's aura. Let us look at a simple exercise that should help you develop clairsentience. To perform this exercise, you will require a quiet space and some free and uninterrupted time.

- Start by being seated in a comfortable position. You can sit on a chair that offers ergonomic support with your feet firmly grounded on the floor. Keep your eyes closed and pay attention to your breathing pattern. Feel the air entering your body through the nostrils, moving through your body, and leaving it. Continue this for a little while to ground yourself.

- While keeping your eyes closed, bring your hands together and rub your palms briskly for about twenty-thirty seconds.
- Extend your hands frontward while keeping your elbows tightly bent and your palm facing each other at about one foot apart.
- Move your hands closer together slowly and pay attention to what you feel or sense in the space between your palms.
- Repeat this process while slowly drawing your hands closer and drawing them apart. Continue to do so while keeping your eyes closed. If you sense any distractions, ground yourself by focusing on your breath again. Pay attention to your breath and the air entering your body and leaving it. This is very effective in grounding you and stabilizing your attention.
- Repeat the hand movements while keeping a close eye on the different sensations, feelings, visualizations, and thoughts that might start running through your psyche. What do you notice during this exercise in the space between your hands?
- Does the sensation or feeling change when you draw your hands further apart or bring them closer to each other?

The best part about this exercise is that there is nothing definitively correct or incorrect. What you experience is your unique reality, and your observations may vary depending on your perceptions and the state of your aura. With time and practice, you will develop a stronger clairsentience, and your ability to feel auras will become better, so much so that you will be able to perform it while keeping your eyes wide open.

Chapter 7: Self-Healing Techniques

In this chapter, you will learn self-healing techniques with hand positions; focus on techniques that address physical symptoms, like a tightness in a certain part of the body or tension or pain.

When you start your journey with Reiki, you will have to begin by practicing on yourself before you try to heal others. You can only heal others once *you* are emotionally and physically healed. This will allow your body to accept the energy of Reiki so you can channel it. Many people take courses to learn about Reiki healing, but it is possible to learn it by yourself. Any beginner can use this book to learn self-healing through Reiki and ways to heal others. If you find this difficult, do not hesitate to sign up for a course held by professionals. Focus on finding the best way to take your journey with Reiki to the next level.

Connecting With the Energy of Reiki

To connect with Reiki energy, you must achieve a higher state of consciousness. In this heightened state, you will have an increased awareness that you are connected to the life energy flowing through the universe. This life energy should flow effortlessly through you. Connecting to the energy of Reiki is the simplest and foremost step, which a lot of beginners find challenging. Even if you struggle to achieve this heightened state, do not get discouraged. For those who practice meditation regularly or have experience in meditation, it can be much easier to accomplish this first step.

Connecting to the energy of the universe will involve two steps. One is that you must let go of any ego and open yourself to the wisdom and the energy flowing through the universe. When you allow yourself to be an open conduit for this energy, you can try visualizing the flow of the energy through you.

You will connect with the universe's consciousness when you achieve the state of mind, which helps you connect with Reiki energy. For Reiki invocation, you simply have to speak to the universe and seek permission to use its energy for healing. You need to be calm and have clarity in your mind while speaking to the universe. To achieve this state of mind, try meditating for a few minutes before a Reiki invocation. It will help you relax and increase your ability to connect with the consciousness of the universe.

As a beginner, you can choose to speak out loud or silently while you do all this. You can ask the universe to connect you to its energy in any way you want. Your personal beliefs will usually guide you to choose a particular way. The common goal should always be that you can heal in a pure holistic way with unconditional love.

Take some time to decide how you want to speak to the universe and what you want to say. Then sit in a quiet place and place your palms together. Your hands should be placed in a prayer position in front of the heart chakra. Healing needs to come from a place of love; this is why the heart chakra is suitable. Once you are ready in this position, you can say something like this:

"I am calling out to the energy of the universe and that of every Reiki conduit from the past, present, and future to participate in this session of healing. I call upon all the energies to help me create a strong connection with the energy of the universe. I ask for the infinite wisdom that will equip me to channel this universal energy. I ask that the universal energy flows through all of me and that I can use its

power to conduct pure and loving healing. I ask for the knowledge that will help me use and channel this energy in the best way possible. I ask for empowerment from the divine love and blessings of the universe."

Asking for permission from the universe is essential for Reiki healing. Do not focus on yourself or have an ego that makes you think that you are solely capable of healing. You have to be in line with the energy of the universe for it to flow through your body so you can act as a channel for healing. Your consciousness must be higher, and your vibrational energy needs to be increased.

Pay attention to the way you speak and ask for permission to become a conduit. It means that you will be asking for permission to become a conductor of the wisdom and knowledge of the universe instead of asking to become a healer or making decisions on your own. This will only be possible if you let go of your ego and allow your beliefs to be aligned with the consciousness of the universe.

Universal energy is not visible to the naked eye since it exists beyond the physical realm. This is why you can connect with it only if your mind is in a heightened state of consciousness. To "see" it, you have to visualize. Visualization will help you feel a physical connection with the energy of the universe. Close your eyes and take a deep breath in.

When you let go of this breath, imagine some blue-white colored energy beams surrounding you. Visualize these beams like threads stretching from the ground to the sky and into the rest of the universe. You will be able to feel this energy as you visualize. Then take another breath in. While letting a deep breath out, focus the energy on your palms, and speak out to the universal energy. When you breathe, take the infinite light in and call for it on your palms as you visualize the energy entering inside your body.

While the energy flows through your body and out from your palms, visualize the cool white energy glowing on your palms. As you do this, you will feel the energy of the universe as it radiates through your palms.

When you employ the tool of visualization, you should remember that it does not matter what you imagine the energy as. You can imagine it in any color or form. The goal is for it to help you feel that energy. It doesn't matter if you cannot see the energy. What matters is your willingness and willpower to connect with it. You will be able to heal with the universe's energy when your thoughts and will are aligned so you can act as a conduit.

Scanning the Aura

Most people have an incorrect perception of how auras exist. Your aura is not some visible energy or something that your body creates. Aura is, in fact, the energy of the universe. It is the energy surrounding every living thing and is not really "around" them like many people imagine. A person's aura exists within the body, too, so it's not just projected outward. Your aura is a part of the energy system in you. It works as the brain as it takes in and puts out information. It can receive and transmit signals from the world around you.

The health of your aura is determined by everything within you. This is why your aura may appear like a dark blob when you have many negative thoughts. We have already explained that auras can have different colors as they transmit information about your body and mind. They can also have varied shapes, sizes, patterns, or textures. Your aura is not always a solid color. When there are discolorations, or there is texture, there will be variations in colors.

When a person connects to the energy of the universe, they can feel the energy around them. If you want to visualize this energy, close your eyes, and place your hands just above your head. Keep your palms facing toward your body. You can use both of your hands or your dominant hand for this exercise. While holding your hands up in this position, keep them about three-six inches away from your body.

Now you will be moving your hands down from your head to the rest of your body. As you pass the different chakras in your body, you can stop for a while. Paying attention to each chakra in this way will help you understand any blemish or imbalance in your aura. As you move your hands down your body for the first time, do a quick sweep from the top until your hips. The root chakra is the lowest energy point at the base of your spine.

Pay attention to how you feel so you can gauge your energy. When you do another pass down your body, pay closer attention to how certain areas feel. In some places, you might find the energy to be lighter or heavier. It will affect the speed in how your hand passes through that area. For instance, your hand may move faster where the energy is lighter and get slower where the energy is thick. You may also sense some subtle differences in temperature or vibrations. In places that feel cooler, the energy is usually flowing out. Where you feel the heat, the energy is mostly being drawn in.

When you notice such differences, your energy probably needs some change or is undergoing change. If you notice this, you have to move on to the next step. As you keep practicing, you will get better with aura scans. With more Reiki sessions, you will be much more in tune with your body and understand what it means so that energy can flow through it freely.

Activation of Reiki Symbols

Reiki symbols, which are made by your hands, help you to transmit energy, heal, and do a lot more. Some symbols are more commonly used than others, and you can use them while healing yourself or another person. Learning these Reiki symbols will help you tap deeper into the power of Reiki. Some of the commonly used symbols you need to familiarize yourself with are:

Distance Symbol

The concept of this symbol can be a little more complex than other Reiki symbols. The Hon Sha Ze Sho Nen symbol stands for peace, enlightenment, and unity. Because this symbol can unify, healers use it while performing Reiki over a distance. The distance symbol can also be used to send attunements over long distances, helping people open their chakras and making them more receptive to the universe's healing energy. Reiki practitioners often use this symbol to send Reiki ahead to a person before they hear some bad news or undergo a difficult situation.

Power Symbol

If you want to decrease or increase your power, this is the symbol you must use. The Cho Ku Rei symbol amplifies many things. It can be visualized like a switch that instantly grants the Reiki healer an enhanced ability to heal when it is turned on. Most healers use this symbol when they start a Reiki session as it helps to amplify the healing energy. It also provides spiritual protection, which is needed when the healer connects to another person's aura while healing them. The power symbol is also used to empower other Reiki symbols. It can be used to infuse healing energy into food. This symbol looks like a coil that is drawn clockwise or counterclockwise, and this is representative of the energy moving through the body.

Emotional and Mental Reiki Symbol

Also known as the harmony symbol, it helps to purify energy and restore emotional and mental balance. The Sei He Ki symbol is suitable for healing mental or emotional issues. The energy of well-being and love from the universe is attached to this symbol. It will help your mind to become calmer and relieve addictions or release negative energy. This symbol is usually drawn in the image of a cresting wave or a bird's wing.

Master Symbol

The Dai Ko Myo symbol is considered more powerful than any other symbol used in Reiki. This is also why it is called the master symbol. This sacred symbol is enlightening and nourishing. Reiki masters are usually the only ones who can connect using this symbol. The master symbol can be used to relieve the body from any illness or disease. It can help to heal the soul and bring about great changes in a person's life. Using this symbol brings Reiki healers a little closer to the almighty.

Setting an Intention

You can set your intention simply by stating what you want. Knowing what disruption or blockage your body is experiencing allows you to trace the root of the problem. Having a targeted approach and directing Reiki energy can help you heal specific ailments. Reiki is often used to heal conditions like pain, stress, obesity, trauma, spiritual imbalance, addiction, insomnia, etc. Your intention can be a message that you send out to the aura.

As you communicate with the aura and state the desired result while directing energy toward the outcome, you are more likely to achieve what you want. You have to be clear and strong when sending out your message if you want it to be heard. If the universe grants your request, you will see the intention reflected in your aura and feel the healing. Using Reiki, along with visualization, will make it easier to set your intention. You have to visualize the outcome you want when you set an intention. Think of how this result will improve your life for the better.

Visualize yourself becoming much happier and having a positive mindset. Think of simple things you enjoy, like going out for dinner with your friends or spending quality time with your partner. Visualize any problem or bad feelings leaving your life. If you currently have a problem, think of how it will be once it is resolved. Your visualization has to be very vivid for it to work. Think of how you will feel when your intentions are materialized. You can feel the relief you get when you get rid of any physical or emotional pain.

If you are healing yourself, visualize how your body would feel once that illness leaves your body. If you want to lose weight, think of how you will look or feel once you lose that weight. If you are doing Reiki for someone else, visualize how you will feel if you have successfully healed them. Setting your intention can be impactful when it is combined with visualization. It has many benefits and will increase the strength of your Reiki healing power.

Energy Guidance

A common error many beginners make is that they believe in prioritizing hand positions while neglecting other parts of the process of healing. In fact, it is much more important for you to connect with your higher consciousness as it will help you access the universe's energy. Setting intentions is another important aspect that is often overlooked. Reiki energy can be guided, especially while targeting some specific part of the body.

When you want to direct the energy of Reiki, begin by placing your hands over the part of the body that you want to target. Use the tool of visualization to see and feel the Reiki energy as it flows while you set your intention. This is to be done when you are trying to heal a particular area. To heal the whole body, you must slowly move your hands over the body instead of keeping it still over one part.

While guiding the healing energy of Reiki over the body, you have to state clearly what your intentions are for every individual area. Repeat steps three, four, and five a few times before you close the connection. You will know that you have finished healing when you perform an aura scan and cannot feel any disruption or blockage of energy.

Close the Connection

Another common mistake among beginners is that they fail to close the connection after a Reiki session. This means they do not attempt to close the connection between the universe and themselves or even between themselves and the person they were healing with Reiki. If you don't close this connection, you leave yourself open to negative energy, which could be released from the other person's aura or your aura. You will feel exhausted or ill when you have to carry such negative energy around. To avoid this, closing the connection is important.

To close the connection, you must release any negative energy accumulated within or around you. Visualize this negative energy as it flows out of the body through your palms and is released outward. Imagine and feel it rejuvenating you as the negativity leaves your system.

Connecting with your normal energy will allow you to reconnect with your normal consciousness. Some practitioners also like washing their hands after a Reiki session to eliminate any negative energy left behind on/in their hands.

Chapter 8: Healing Others

Healing others is more of a level two activity, but you can get started with some basic healing techniques at level one. Here you will learn how to prepare for the treatment of others and various beginner-friendly ways you can get started with Reiki healing.

After your first-degree Reiki attunement, you can begin healing others with Reiki. In the first degree of Reiki, you can only heal someone by being near them. But after second-degree Reiki, you can heal people from a distance.

Hands-on Healing

When you want to give Reiki to someone with your hands, ask them to lie down or sit in front of you. Get them comfortable and let them sit/lie in the position that will be most suitable for them and you. They should be in a position that gives you access to every chakra in the body and will allow you to give Reiki conveniently.

When a patient first reaches out to you, let them know that they should wear comfortable clothing for the session. Something loose fitting will be more appropriate than tight, uncomfortable clothing. Before getting ready for the Reiki session, ask them to remove any accessories like their jewelry, watch, or spectacles. Then have a glass of water and offer one to them. Being hydrated is important. Then let them lie down comfortably on their back and ask them to close their eyes.

Begin healing with the crown chakra and continue with the rest of the front chakras.

After this, use spiraling to balance energy. To do this, place your left hand over their right shoulder. Then touch your ring or little finger with your thumb with the other fingers of your right hand extended. Use this hand to draw spirals in an anticlockwise manner from the left shoulder to the left hand. Then start spiraling from the left shoulder to their left foot. After this, do the same from the right shoulder to their right foot and their right shoulder to their right hand.

Once this is done, ask them to turn over onto their stomach from the right side. Then you can begin healing the back chakras.

After this, you must start balancing. Place your hands above their back crown chakra and root chakra. Keep your hands about six inches above their body. Try sensing the energy flow. If you notice any imbalance, use Reiki to restore balance in the energy levels. Then move your hands so they hover over their throat and hara chakras. After balancing these chakras, you can move on to the heart and solar chakras. After these, you should slowly move your hands over their heart chakra and let them rest over their body.

Your left hand should then be placed over the left shoulder of the patient. Form a V shape with the middle and index fingers of your right hand. Using this shape, start drawing a line from their throat chakra to their root chakra. If the person has diabetes, draw this line in the opposite direction from the root to the throat chakra. Let your right hand rest over their back hara chakra. Repeat this three times before you gently wake the patient up.

Distant Healing

When you are attuned to second-degree Reiki, you can try distance healing. If someone wants to receive Reiki from a distance, ask them to set aside time for this session. They should be prepared at the time when you will be sending them Reiki energy. If they are in tune with you during the distance healing session, it will allow them to absorb the energy better and increase the ability to heal.

Ask the patient to sit down comfortably with their feet bare and touching the floor. Ask them to close their eyes and keep their legs and arms uncrossed. Instruct them to keep their mind and heart open to receiving the healing energy through you. They should be able to feel the energy as it comes to them.

There are various ways in which energy can be sent over a distance. Objects can be used as a surrogate, or you can send the energy through your third eye.

Here are some different distant healing techniques:

Use a Photograph

Ask the patient to send you their photograph. You can then send Reiki to this photograph. Drawing Reiki symbols over the back of this photograph will be helpful. You can also write that their problem is solved there. While giving Reiki, hold the photograph between your palms. Imagine the Reiki symbols while conducting the session.

Use Your Imagination

You do not always need a physical object to replace the person. Bring your palms together and imagine that person to be within your palms or lying in front of you. Then start giving them energy through your imagination and let them bathe in that Reiki energy. Imagine that they are healed and feeling better.

Use a Surrogate

An object like a stuffed toy can be used as a surrogate for the person receiving Reiki. In your mind, declare that the object represents the patient before you begin giving it Reiki. If the real patient has a specific part to which they want treatment targeted, you can perform the same on the object accordingly. If not, you can give Reiki to the entire body of the object the same way you would to a real person. In fact, you can even use your thumb as a surrogate and enclose it within your palms as you give it Reiki for the patient.

Use Your Third Eye

If you can visualize that person, you can use your third eye. Visualize Reiki energy coming out from your third eye chakra and going toward that person. Imagine the energy like a beam of healing light and use that beam to draw Reiki symbols on that person. The third eye can be used if you imagine them before you or have a picture of them with you.

Consent

Consent is an important aspect of giving Reiki to someone else. Many people are doubtful about whether they can send Reiki energy to a person without asking for their permission. Asking for consent is important because it will allow them to open themselves up to receiving the energy you send

When there is consent, Reiki is effective, and healing takes place much more quickly. In fact, without consent, healing may not happen at all.

Use an Intention Slip

An intention box is a small box where you can keep some rolled-up papers. Write down your intentions on these papers and put them inside the box. While writing intentions, it is important to use affirmative language and nothing negative. Do not use negative words like "Don't" or "No." Avoid using any full stops as well. At the end of the intention, write, "Thank you, Reiki. It is so, and it will be done." The paper should not be folded but rolled up and put inside. Using a Reiki box can allow you to give Reiki to more than one person at once. Just hold the box between your hands and mentally draw Reiki symbols on it as you give it Reiki. It is not necessary to think of each individual separately while doing this Reiki session.

Healing Tips from Reiki Masters

It takes years of practice for Reiki Masters to navigate and understand the subtle energy shifts involved in Reiki. However, they say that anyone can learn to work with energy and heal others with Reiki. Practice is essential for improving your skills, but you do not need ten years under your belt to begin giving Reiki to others. Just keep the following tips in mind when you use Reiki on others:

1. The first step is to receive energy. Before you give Reiki to someone else, you must activate the Chi within you first. Sit comfortably and close your eyes. As you take some deep breaths, imagine a stream of white healing light flowing from the crown of your head, through to your heart, and out through your arms and hands. Ask the universe to heal you before you heal the person before you. Once you start feeling the flow of energy, envision yourself healing the other person. Keep coming back to your breath if you get distracted.

2. Reiki is great for helping others sleep. For this, you need to ask the person to lie down comfortably. Stand or sit near their head. Now visualize a healing stream of light passing from your hands into their crown as this light gets rid of any discomfort or pain they may have experienced that day. Tell them to take a few deep breaths in and out. Ask them to think about the whole day that passed and tell them to thank each aspect of the day and let it go. As you channel the Reiki energy through your palms, allow them to go to sleep slowly. Visualize their mind and body relaxing and being healed as it slowly gets heavy with sleep.

3. Reiki can also help relieve stress. Stress and anxiety can cause breathing problems. By placing your hands over the person's shoulders before you, you can channel Reiki through them. As you give them Reiki, their mental energy becomes less intense, and they slowly calm down.

4. After every Reiki session, remember to seal off the energy. Offer gratitude to the universe and do a cleansing on yourself. After you finish healing the person, close off the energy path. This can be done simply by moving away from them and wiping or washing any excess energy off your hands. Place your hands together in prayer position and thank the Reiki energy, yourself, and the person before you.

Chapter 9: Receiving Your First Reiki Attunement

In this chapter, we get onto the topic of Reiki attunements, what they are and why they are necessary. This cannot be done through a book, but *this* book equips you with the knowledge needed to receive the first initiation into traditional Usui Reiki. Do not follow questionable Reiki masters on the Internet and always ask for proof of the master's lineage when you do. You will also get tips on how to best prepare for this first attunement and what can be expected during a Reiko attunement—once the right master is found.

A Reiki master passes the art down to their student through an attunement. You cannot become a true Reiki practitioner if you have not been attuned.

What Is a Reiki Attunement?

Attunements are also called empowerments by some healers. In Usui Reiki or that of Tibetan lineage, there are two types of attunements. One attunement method is for those who want to use Reiki for self-healing or healing others. The other attunement is for those who want to get healed by a Reiki healer. Here you will learn about the first type of attunement, which is used by people who want to heal themselves or others with Reiki.

The Reiki Master Teacher transfers their ability to channel the energy of Reiki to their student during the attunement process, otherwise known as the Reiju. Reiju is a sacred initiation that connects you with the Reiki source. You do not have to do anything special other than being open and willing to learn to receive this energy.

Rei is the universal consciousness, and during the attunement, it will adjust your chakras, aura, and energy channels, allowing energy to flow freely. The process of attunement will create a permanent channel between the Reiki energy and you. This channel runs from the top of your head through all the energy channels within you. At the heart chakra, the energy will branch out and flow into your palm chakras through your arms. It also goes down to your root chakra and further down through your legs to the bottom of your feet. As the energy flows out through the chakras in your feet, you become a conduit for this spiritual energy.

When you receive a Reiki attunement, it will start a cleansing process for your entire being. For most people, it takes about twenty-one days to be completely cleansed. There may be a period of processing where certain areas of your life have to be adjusted to accommodate such new conditions.

Many students have claimed to experience these common symptoms after their first Reiki attunements.

- A cleansing process begins in the physical body. Toxins accumulated within the body are brought out to the surface and removed. Foods you may have had cravings for will not seem as appetizing anymore. You may feel like your body needs more rest.

- If you have any long-suppressed emotions, they might start coming to the surface. You may experience intense anger, grief, or any such emotion that you might have held in for a while.

- The cleansing process may occur in your mind and release any limiting or old beliefs and thought patterns. You can either reject or accept certain situations in your mind. The law of attraction will play an important role, so you have to consider what thoughts you want to materialize in your life.
- The cleansing in your spirit or astral body will allow any stagnant and negative energy to be released. It will cleanse your aura and make your connection with the universe much stronger as spiritual lessons start becoming important again.

If you read or ask about the experiences of other people who have received Reiki attunements, it will further convince you to try it. Receiving an attunement can help you connect with the most powerful and beautiful healing energy in the universe. This energy will play a prominent role throughout your life.

Preparing for the First Attunement

Attunement is the process where the Reiki master uses their hands to redirect energy and open the chakras in a person. The levels of attunement will vary depending on the class. The three classes are the first, second, and third level. With attunements, the energetic pathways in a person's body are cleared up, allowing the Reiki energy to flow freely through them. This helps put right any mental or physical issues that may have resulted from blocked energy.

It is also important to understand that not all Reiki attunements are equal. Some people do not notice or experience any discomfort or difference after an attunement. Some will notice a subtle change, and others might experience a very significant adjustment. When there is a big adjustment, it can be a little unsettling and takes some getting used to.

According to experts, it is recommended that a person undergo a purification period before their attunement.

This will help the attunement process and reduce discomfort, which might be experienced after the attunement. A Reiki attunement should not be taken lightly. When you take a few precautionary steps, it will truly allow you to benefit from a Reiki attunement.

The following are some suggested preparations before attunements:

- Be careful about selecting the right Reiki teacher or practitioner.
- Schedule the Reiki attunement session well in advance. Don't leave it until the last minute and show up without any preparation.
- Don't consume any alcohol in the week before the attunement.
- If you are on any medication, continue with it as usual.
- If you smoke, try to reduce smoking as much as possible or avoid it the day before, during, and after the attunement.
- Try fasting for a day or two before the attunement. You can fast on water or try a juice cleanse.
- About three days or more before your Reiki attunement, reduce or eliminate the amount of fish, meat, or poultry you consume.
- Avoid any outside stimulation from the radio, TV, or computer for a while.
- Take some time to meditate and spend time with nature if you can. Some periods of solitude will be beneficial before the attunement.
- Stay hydrated by drinking a lot of water.
- Do an aura cleanse before the Reiki attunement.
- On the night before the attunement, go to bed early. Getting some good rest is recommended. If you have not been fasting, consume a very light breakfast before the session.
- Avoid doing things that will deplete too much of your energy. Be gentle with yourself.

Tips for Increasing the Effectiveness of the Attunement

- During the period before and after the attunement, it is recommended that you pray or connect with the universe daily.
- Prepare yourself for a twenty-one-day period of cleansing after the attunement.
- If you intend to get the attunement done at a place that is far from home, prepare a place to stay near the center where it will take place. You might not feel up for a long journey after the session. The Reiki center might have rooms, or you can always book a motel or hotel room for the night.
- If you take medication for any illness, go back to the doctor for a re-evaluation after the twenty-one-day period following the attunement. The attunement might have helped clear a lot of bad energy, and you might need less medication than before.

How to Find a Qualified Reiki Healer?

There are quite a few ways through which you can find a qualified Reiki practitioner.

1. Ask a relative or friend who does Reiki. Reiki is not the same as other healing methods you are used to. You do not have to go to a professional, like a doctor, to receive Reiki. There are no credentials or prerequisites to receive training for Reiki. Reiki originated as a holistic folk practice. You can turn to a friend, relative, or acquaintance trained in Reiki who practices it regularly for your attunement process. If the first Reiki session with them feels right for you, you can continue with them or ask them to connect you with their Reiki Master.

2. Look for someone in your community. Ask around at your local yoga studios or health food stores. Word of mouth is usually important for such businesses, and they tend to recommend each other. Such places will be able to lead you in the right direction for a local Reiki practitioner. Look up lists of community resources and ask at medical centers that offer holistic or integrative medicine.

3. Find a professional who practices Reiki. These days, many practitioners have set up legitimate Reiki healthcare centers. You can look up reviews online and search for the best practitioner in your area. In fact, there are a lot of medical units that incorporate Reiki healing in their practice as well. In 2007, more than 800 hospitals in the United States offered Reiki services to their patients. If you are being treated for other medical issues at such hospitals, you can always ask them to set up a Reiki session for you.

Evaluating Their Qualifications

So, you have found a Reiki practitioner, but how can you tell if they are qualified? Reiki is not a practice that is taught like some academic medical courses. It is taught in different ways by different people and is more of a grassroots movement. You cannot gauge the qualifications of a Reiki master through standards like education. Having a certificate is not a guarantee that the person will have had sufficient practice. You must ask certain questions and make your own judgments to decide if they are the right Reiki practitioner for you.

Check to see if they have enough experience. They should have been practicing for some time and not be someone who has just started or practices irregularly. The more practice the healer has had, the better the healing session will go. When you look up professional practitioners, look for their training and practice details in their brochures or websites.

Here are some questions you should ask and the answers you should look for:

- What is their level of training? Reiki can be received from someone regardless of their level of training. For distance healing, it is better to turn toward a second-degree Reiki practitioner, whereas a Reiki master is needed to learn how to practice Reiki yourself.

- When were they trained? Learning when they were trained will tell you how long they have been practicing Reiki. Another determinant is how often they practice. They might have received the training a long time ago but not have practiced for years. Someone who practices daily is much more ideal than an infrequent practitioner.

- What was the length of the classes? For the first degree, eight or twelve hours are enough, while second-degree training requires another eight or twelve hours. This gives enough time for instruction and practice during classes. When classes are carried out over two-three days, it allows more practice time.

- Were the levels taught in separate classes, and how far apart were these classes? This is something you must ask Reiki masters or second-degree practitioners. The training for the second degree should ideally be done within three-six months of the first-degree training. This allows the practitioner to get a lot of practice before moving on to more advanced healing techniques. In some cases, Reiki masters will require their students to practice for at least a year before they come for the second-degree classes. After this, the student should take a couple of years to get more hands-on practice before attempting to become a Reiki master. The more traditional Reiki masters require their students to gain much more experience than this.

- What is their practical healing experience? How many years have they been practicing healing for, and whom have they treated? When you look for a professional practitioner, check to see if they have at least a few years of experience giving Reiki to people beyond their close circle of friends and family. Look for someone who has healed people with various issues and helped them regain good health.

• How do they describe Reiki? The professional practitioner should give you a satisfactory answer to this question. If they hesitate and act like they have not given it a thought before now, you should probably go elsewhere. An experienced Reiki healer will have clarity and explain it confidently. While Reiki healing is very helpful, it does not act as a substitute for other medical care. Be careful about relying on a practitioner who tells you to stay away from conventional healthcare and claims to cure any disease you have. When you ask a practitioner what Reiki means to them, it gives you a good sense of them and their experience.

• How long are their sessions, and how much do they charge? Find a practitioner who will explain the process and details. They should let you know how they intend to conduct the sessions and what it will involve. Ask them if they will include anything other than Reiki in their sessions and specify if Reiki is all you seek. Asking about the fees is important so that you know what to expect and if you will get your money's worth. Those with more experience and longer sessions tend to charge more. Most Reiki practitioners charge a very low fee, so it is an affordable option.

• Do they practice Reiki every day? This is an important question, and the answer should be "yes." A Reiki healer should be someone who integrates Reiki into their everyday life. It allows them to build their healing skills and ensure their personal health before healing someone else.

These questions can easily be asked before you begin with someone. They are reasonable, and any good practitioner should be willing to answer through an email or on the phone, even if it is not face-to-face. It will show you their credibility and help you decide if you should trust them in the first place.

Chapter 10: Reiki for Daily Well-being

The Reiki tips in this section can be turned into daily habits to encourage optimal health and well-being. For instance, you could recite the principles as daily prayer, try self-healing daily, create Reiki Water and drink it first thing every morning, etc. You should seek a Reiki Master for attunement purposes as well.

After you have received the first Reiki attunement, practicing Reiki every day will be a great benefit. When you practice daily, it helps keep your chakras aligned and opens your energy paths so you can heal others. It will also allow you to direct the flow of Reiki energy consciously.

Habits to Improve Your Reiki Practice

Be More Open to Change

Routine can be comforting, but change is also necessary. With change, you get to evolve emotionally, spiritually, and intellectually. Keep switching things up, and you can liven up your daily routine and learn a lot more as you go on.

Volunteer to Help Others

Reiki is a practice of compassion and kindness. Even if you are a professional practitioner, take the opportunity to help people for free at times. Volunteer at hospitals or animal shelters. It will allow you to keep honing your Reiki practice and give you the chance to give back to the universe.

Use Your Heart to See

At times, having an open heart can be difficult, but it is also crucial for a Reiki practitioner. Seeing things from your heart and not your eyes is an integral part of Reiki. When you are healing someone, focus on their inner light rather than thinking too much about their suffering. Your intentions and Reiki skills will help them get better.

Keep Learning

There is no end to the knowledge you can accumulate about Reiki. Read more books, attend lectures, or just follow blogs of other Reiki practitioners. You will always learn something new.

Here Are Some Easy Ways to Practice Reiki Daily

Start Your Day with Reiki

Do not reach for your phone as soon as you wake up. Starting the day with such activities only sets a negative tone for the rest of the day. If you begin with a little Reiki, it allows healing energy to keep you going all day.

Be Purposeful about How You Respond to Pain

When we have a headache, our fingers automatically reach out to the point of pain, and we press around it to relieve the pain. Now you can do better by practicing Reiki. Use your whole hand to cover the pain, allowing the healing energy to flow.

Practice Reiki with Yoga

Yoga is a great way to keep your body and mind healthy. If you add some Reiki exercises to your daily yoga practice, not only will your physical body improve, but you will also see a difference in the state of your mind and spirit.

Do Some Reiki While You Are in the Shower?

When you take a shower, you use your hands to cleanse your body with soap. Go one step further and take a little extra time to perform Reiki all over your body after cleaning. It will keep your body cleansed from outside and within.

Do Some Reiki When You Are Stuck in Traffic or Just Traveling

Instead of getting bad-tempered when you're stuck in traffic, take this time to do some Reiki. Similarly, if you have any time during your commute to work, you can do the same. It will be the perfect pick-me-up and make you feel better than a cup of coffee.

These easy steps will help you incorporate Reiki into your daily life. The more Reiki you practice, the better you get at it, and the more it benefits you.

Conclusion

Hopefully, you found this Reiki guide useful and interesting. The information should be immensely useful for any beginner wanting to learn the practice of Reiki.

Starting today, watch as you slowly begin to master the art of this holistic healing method. It is important that you begin Reiki with an open mind and heart. It will only work if you let go of your skepticism and prejudice. Although you might not see any visible results from the practices mentioned here at first, it is important to keep trying.

With a little practice, you can get much better at Reiki healing in a short time. Daily Reiki can help you get rid of energy imbalances or blockages and promote well-being. You can keep referring to this book as you practice, and it will help you eventually master Reiki healing every day.

Good luck and good health.

Here's another book by Mari Silva that you might like

Your Free Gift (only available for a limited time)

Thanks for getting this book! If you want to learn more about various spirituality topics, then join Mari Silva's community and get a free guided meditation MP3 for awakening your third eye. This guided meditation mp3 is designed to open and strengthen ones third eye so you can experience a higher state of consciousness. Simply visit the link below the image to get started.

https://spiritualityspot.com/meditation

Bibliography

Alternativa-za-vas.com. "Palm Healing." Accessed October 1, 2021. https://alternativa-za-vas.com/en/index.php/clanak/article/palm-healing

Baron, Marci. "What Everyone Should Know About Energy Healing." mindbodygreen. March 1, 2016. https://www.mindbodygreen.com/0-23890/what-everyone-should-know-about-energy-healing.html

Bourne, Robert. "Scanning the Aura in Reiki Healing." *YouTube* video, 2:55. August 5, 2009. https://www.youtube.com/watch?v=WwCpvxYCkVk

Cameron, Yogi. "A Beginner's Guide To The 7 Chakras." mindbodygreen. October 29, 2021. https://www.mindbodygreen.com/0-91/The-7-Chakras-for-Beginners.html

CA SHEFALI RASTOGI. "Reiki level 1 self-healing." *YouTube* video, 17:07. October 9, 2019. https://www.youtube.com/watch?v=rxxADnfhh40

Dale, Cyndi. "Energetic Anatomy: A Complete Guide to the Human Energy Fields & Etheric Bodies." Conscious Lifestyle Magazine. October 11, 2016. https://www.consciouslifestylemag.com/human-energy-field-aura/

Desy, Phylameana. lila. "How To Prepare for Your Reiki Attunement." Learn Religions. May 10, 2019. https://www.learnreligions.com/prepare-for-Reiki-attunement-1725329

Dimancea, Vlad. "What Are The Reiki Hand Positions And How To Use Them." ReikiScoop. November 9, 2019. https://Reikiscoop.com/what-are-the-Reiki-hand-positions-and-how-to-use-them/

Estrada, Jessica. "We're All a Little Psychic—Here Are 4 Ways to Develop That Intuitive Muscle. Well+Good. February 25, 2020. https://www.wellandgood.com/how-to-develop-psychic-abilities/

Hausauer, Nancy. "Sensing Chakras: A How-To for New Energy Healers." Accessed October 1, 2021. https://www.the-energy-healing-site.com/sensing-chakras.html

Herron, David. "Traditional hand positions for Reiki treatment." October 19, 2015. https://thereikipage.com/handpos.html

icrtofficial. "Reiki Hand Positions for Treating Others. *YouTube* video, 5:33. October 10, 2007. https://www.youtube.com/watch?v=Xw9EleHuXsI

Jessica. "20 Clairvoyant Exercises and Tips (Cheat Sheet)." Intuitive Souls Blog. April 30, 2019. https://intuitivesoulsblog.com/clairvoyant-exercises/

Lee, Ilchi. "Did You Know You Can Sense Energy? Here's How." Change Your Energy. October 31, 2013. https://www.changeyourenergy.com/blog/712/did-you-know-you-can-sense-energy-heres-how

Lübeck, Walter. "Basics of Reiki-Chakra Work." The International Center for Reiki Training. January 7, 2003. https://www.reiki.org/articles/basics-Reiki-chakra-work

McKinnley, Trish. "What is an Energy Ball & How do I Create One?" October 30, 2019. https://www.trishmckinnley.com/how-to-create-an-energy-ball/

McNally, Roseleen. "Reiki Hand Positions." The Thirsty Soul. February 24, 2014. https://www.thethirstysoul.com/Reiki-hand-positions/

Mind Body Soul. "5 Minute Chakra Balance Guided Meditation for Positive Energy And Deep Healing|Unblock all 7 Chakras." *YouTube* video, 7:03. July 20, 2019. https://www.youtube.com/watch?v=tdT1o4gqejA

Moone, Aurora. "5 Easy Ways To Practice Reiki Everyday." Plentiful Earth. August 28, 2016. https://plentifulearth.com/5-easy-ways-practice-Reiki-everyday/

MyGaiany. "The history of Reiki – Usui Reiki." February 8, 2017. http://mygaiany.com/2017/02/history-Reiki-usui-Reiki/

Orgone Energy Australia. "7 Steps to a Chakra Cleansing (To Perform on Yourself or Someone Else)." September 17, 2019. https://www.orgoneenergy.org/blogs/news/chakra-cleansing

Prasad, Kathleen. "8 habits for improving your daily Reiki practice." Animal Reiki Source. June 23, 2017. https://www.animalreikisource.com/8-habits-improving-daily-Reiki-practice/

Regents of the University of Minnesota. "How Can I Find a Qualified Reiki Practitioner?" Accessed October 1, 2021. https://www.takingcharge.csh.umn.edu/explore-healing-practices/Reiki/how-can-i-find-qualified-Reiki-practitioner

Shape editors. "The Beginner's Guide to Meditation." Meredith Corporation. September 8, 2021. https://www.shape.com/lifestyle/mind-and-body/beginners-guide-meditation

Share, Taylor. "How To Start Meditating: The Ultimate Guide For Beginner's Meditation." Nerd Fitness. December 10, 2020. https://www.nerdfitness.com/blog/meditation-building-the-superpower-you-didnt-even-know-you-had/

Stiene, Bronwen, and Stiene, Frans. *The Japanese Art of Reiki*. Winchester, UK: O Books, 2005.

Teal Swan. "How To See Auras -Teal Swan-" *YouTube* video, 26:53. November 2, 2014. https://www.youtube.com/watch?v=2GUhqQAE4UQ

Tru-Life | Carla Trujillo. "Reiki Self-Treatment | How to Give Yourself a Reiki Self Healing | How to Reiki Video Tutorial." *YouTube* video, 8:48. February 8, 2012. https://www.youtube.com/watch?v=f_7TXfQJL2Y

Vogel, Kaitlin. "What's Your Aura? Learn All About Aura Meaning, Colors, Cleansing and How to Read Them." YogiApproved. October 28, 2019. https://www.yogiapproved.com/om/aura-meaning/

Wicks, Rosemarie. "Holistic Healing Explained." School of Natural Health Sciences. June 2, 2016. https://naturalhealthcourses.com/2016/06/holistic-healing-explained/

Printed in Great Britain
by Amazon